# Foster Parenting Matters

### Creating a Home for Hope and Healing

## Julie Bagamary

Edited by Patricia Lockard

Cover and book design by Meghan McDonald

Cover art by Julie Bagamary

Printed in the United States of America

First Printing, 2021

ISBN 978-0-578-82184-9

Dedicated to

foster parents -

past, current, future,

and those who support them.

# CONTENTS

# PREFACE

Like many little girls, I dreamed of one day marrying a wonderful man, having children and living happily ever after together. I think somewhere along my way to adulthood, I lost sight of that dream. So, when I met Randy in the fall of 1978, I thought it was too good to be true. We both worked at a resort hotel in south Florida. I was parking fancy cars for the dinner theater club after my college classes working toward a degree as an optometric technician and he was working as a front desk clerk. We got to know each other briefly each night after my shift when I turned in keys to the front desk for the cars whose owners who were still in the club. I often would go back to the break room and get him a grape soda before driving back to my apartment.

He was a gentle yet strong young man who treated me with respect. And he was so cute! He seemed adventurous, yet very shy. I don't think I've ever been shy. Almost every report card of mine from elementary school had "talks too much" in the comments. I think it should have read "very friendly" instead but no one ever asked me. After a few weeks working together, Randy needed a date for an event at the dinner theater club where he was to accompany one of the other managers. Randy asked me to be his date. My grandfather had just died and the event night was the same night I was traveling across the state with my brother to the funeral. We chuckle now about how I said I couldn't go because my grandfather died. "Really, it's true but I'd like to go another time." I wasn't sure Randy believed me still when we hung up the phone.

Thankfully Randy asked me for a date again a few weeks later and I accepted. On the fourth of March we had our first date at the same dinner theater club where we worked. It was a fun time in one of the most elegant places I had ever been in to eat. Going in and out of the lobby of the dinner club for my valet parking job, allowed me to pass by some of the famous entertainers but I had never attended an actual show. Randy had a tender steak and I had a saucy duck à la orange. Randy was very quiet and I talked a lot. I don't remember who the entertainer was for the evening. On our third date, Randy asked me to marry him! Although we were becoming very close quickly, I was shocked. I was scared really. Marriage is such a huge commitment and I wasn't sure I was ready. With mixed emotions, after my classes ended for the semester, I packed my belongings and moved back to my parents' home town across the state for the summer.

Randy and I continued to talk a lot on the phone and I realized that I indeed loved him. One night while talking on the phone, I said "Yes, I will marry you." Three weeks after my moving back home to my parent's house,

I returned to my college town and found an apartment. Randy officially gave me an engagement ring on the thirty first of May and we began discussing possible wedding dates. Due to my class schedule, holidays etc., we kept moving the wedding date up until we decided that July would work – only six weeks away. Pre-marital counseling was a requirement of the pastor at the church where we were being married and one of the questions he asked us was how many children we planned to have. Randy, knowing that I would say the typical two, said six. The pastor suggested a good compromise would be four, which was exactly what Randy was hoping the pastor would say. So, we chuckled that four children would become our plan and in reality, it did. We were married in July 1979 and camped along the Blue Ridge Parkway for our honeymoon.

We loved it in the mountains and joked that we were just going to send for our things and stay there. After returning home, Randy went back to work at the resort hotel and I finished my last year of school and worked in optometry. We actually did began making plans to move to the mountains where we had honeymooned as soon as possible.

Our first child, a healthy girl, was born in August 1980. We were delighted and loved being parents. Four months later, with our small baby, we moved to Asheville, North Carolina, near the Blue Ridge Parkway as we had dreamed of and planned for.

It was the coldest place I had ever lived. We were on a new adventure geographically far from all that was familiar. Later that year, I had a miscarriage that emotionally rocked me to my core. Randy was working many, many hours at a prestigious hotel in town and I often felt like a single parent. Our daughter was/is strong willed which is really a gift once it's focused in a good direction but can be difficult in the process. I was really struggling especially since we had moved away from all our family and it seemed no one was out and about in the wintertime in our new area. I felt very alone and was overwhelmed with grief. Even though my doctor assured me that miscarriages were more common than I realized, I struggled thinking that I must have done something to cause it. Maybe I wasn't a good parent after all. I can see now that that was not true but at the time it was over-whelming. I remembered that my birth mom who died when I was thirteen had had many physical challenges and miscarriages. For a short time, I declared that I never again wanted to get pregnant and risk experiencing the pain of losing another child.

Thankfully, I changed that declaration and had a re-newed mindset. I later gave birth to three healthy children, all boys, in 1982, 1984 and 1985. Our little family was complete. Although I greatly enjoyed being a mom and Randy being a dad, having four children is both exhilarat-ing and challenging and I felt four was my limit. That was the plan anyway, right?

As our children grew, we often had their friends over to our home to play, for meals, and sleep overs. Randy coached our children and their teams in soccer and baseball. We supported our children with our presence at their music, school and sporting events. We were very involved in their lives. It seemed throughout the years we had our four children at home, we also had many of their friends there as well. We loved having lots of people at our home. Even after our children grew up and went to college, we supported them in the times they spoke at events, played sports, etc. They each knew they could bring home friends from college as long as they gave me a heads up so I could prepare for meals. Having children that were not biologically ours in our home had become normal for us and we liked it that way.

# Introduction

In August 2005, Category 5 Hurricane Katrina hit New Orleans, Louisiana, hard.

Most of the city was underwater, causing great structural damage and many lives were lost. Watching it on the news was heart breaking.

Along with the federal government, countless private relief organizations and ministries from across the United States and even Europe began offering aid. Large quantities of water bottles, food, blankets, emergency medical kits, and clean up supplies were being sent to help those trying to recover from such devastation. Many churches formed mission teams to go and help organize supplies to be given out and to rebuild homes and structures. Ministry teams also went to offer emotional and spiritual support.

My church was creating a team to help wherever needed, along with collecting necessary funds. Although we had contributed financially to the team, I knew I wanted to help out more.

I discerned that physically going there with all the mold was not a good choice for me. As I continued to pray about how to help, nothing seemed to come to mind.

A few days later, I mentioned this to Randy, who causally said that he wondered if there were children who had lost both parents and needed to be adopted. Surprised, I said, "Let's send water or food." Adoption or foster parenting was not consciously on my radar at that time—at all!

I'm not sure I really even knew a family that was foster parenting at that time. And I only personally knew a couple families that had adopted babies due to infertility.

That conversation began a process entertaining the question of what *was* the Lord calling us to do for those affected by Hurricane Katrina. But adoption—no way! Even as I write this, I am tearing up remembering the fear and disbelief I felt that the Lord would ask that of us. Hadn't we almost finished raising our four children, teaching them of the Lord and His ways? Our youngest son, Tim was a freshman in college and we were enjoying going to watch him play for the school's football team. We had released each of our children into the world to have and raise families of their own. I'd heard for so many years that four children were plenty. So many had told us that it was "our time" now. Yet, there was this unsettledness in my heart that knew the Lord wanted more and I flat out told Him that I wouldn't do it! I am not proud of that. I am just being honest.

Fast forward a few months when my women's small group was going to a Women of Faith event weekend. Even though I wasn't sure I wanted to go, I did. Someone else had backed out and offered me their already-paid-for ticket. I remember so clearly that Saturday at the event.

I had gone downstairs to look for the prayer room and gotten lost in the huge event arena while trying to find it. I overheard an announcement that Bible study, author and teacher, Beth Moore was about to speak and I didn't want to miss it. I decided to head back upstairs to rejoin my group in the main arena. But I got lost again and couldn't find my way back to my group. A good sense of direction is not one of my strongest qualities. Somehow, I ended up in an overflow room with women I had never met. I chose to stay and listen, planning to rejoin my group after Beth spoke. Beth was speaking on Joshua 1:9 about how the Israelites had to step *into* the water of the Jordan River before it would part for them to cross. Beth ended her talk by inviting each of us to stand up and together take a step forward. As I did just that, my feet felt actually wet. So much so, that I looked down to see if they *were wet*. I felt the Lord say to me, "I am going to ask you one more time about being a foster parent. Will you obey me?" At that moment, I surrendered to that call—yes, I believe foster parenting is a call. I could barely explain what I had experienced to friends in my group when I eventually met back up with them. I wasn't sure I could explain it to myself. I was crying uncontrollably. I believe partly because the relief of surrender was so great but also because I was so scared of what that surrender would look like. Upon returning home, I reluctantly told Randy about my experience at the Women of Faith weekend. Knowing that the Lord tells both husband and wife when He calls them to do something, I asked Randy what he thought.

To my surprise, Randy said the Lord had already told him that we were to be foster parents and ultimately adopt and that he, Randy, was waiting for the Lord to tell me. That was not the reply I was hoping for.

This book is based on my experience as a trained therapeutic foster parent of twelve years, 2005–2017. Randy and I learned many things along the way. Because you are reading this book, I know that foster parenting is on your mind. Perhaps you have felt called to foster and possibly adopt a child who needs a loving and caring home like yours. Maybe you know a friend or family member who is considering or has already chosen to become a foster or adoptive parent.

My desire in this book is to inspire and help current and future foster parents and those surrounding foster parents with our story. I will share things that worked for us, things that didn't work for us, and, hopefully, my story will spark creative solutions for you on your own journey.

I have written out of some real-life issues that Randy and I experienced to help you sidestep some of the pitfalls that I wish someone had told us to look out for. I want to further inspire, educate, encourage, equip and offer confidence in foster parents at all stages giving you helpful information in one place based on my personal experience. It is also my desire to inspire you to not just offer a home for hurting children. I want to motivate you to be a great foster parent by offering a loving and safe home for children needing excellent care at a traumatic time in their lives. Every family situation is unique and you may hit some of your own pitfalls that you can share with others to aid them and I hope you will do that. Ideas and information shared here can apply to anyone who wants to be a great foster parent, even though I write from my view point as a believer in Christ.

Honestly, I have been so hesitant to write this book. Even when the idea and possible title, "How to Be a Great Foster Parent" was suggested to me by my art and business mentor, Matt Tommey, I thought it was crazy. Matt and his team lead the global Created to Thrive Mentoring group that I had been a part of for two years at the time I am writing this. I had submitted a simple question for the weekly Question and Answer Facebook Live time. I planned to listen to the response live the next day as I drove to meet a friend. I expected a quick and technical "how to" type answer that I intended to add to my goals and then implement them the next week.

My question was about how to publish and charge for my list of *respite guidelines* for foster parents as an e-book. Many foster parents and even related agencies had requested that information from me over the years. Now I had finally put what had worked for us during our foster parenting season into writing and was ready to officially share it with others.

Matt was not only my art and business mentor, he was my friend. So, he already knew much of our foster parenting story. His answer surprised me with other artists from around the globe listening too. Matt spent several minutes talking about how Randy and I had authority in the area of foster parenting. He then encouraged me to not just publish the respite guidelines, but to write a whole book. As I was driving to my friend's house, listening in disbelief, I kept saying out loud, "No, no, no!" A book? Um, I don't think so.

It's not that I hadn't considered sharing more of what we had learned during our foster parenting season with others. I had. I had spoken at a couple conferences for foster and adoptive parents. I had led art workshops with adoption groups, giving them creative tools to help with their emotions. Mostly, I simply shared my experiences with another foster or adoptive parent I already knew or who had been encouraged to call me. Typically, I would share one-on-one with a mom who was trying to make sense of it all.

I considered myself a good foster parent—but great? That was too much. Foster parenting can be a huge blessing to you and the child. It can also be a challenge. As we closed the foster parenting chapter of our lives, I saw a closed and locked door. I didn't realize that my path and story would continue to interact with so many who are considering becoming foster parents, those already foster parents and adoptive parents, as well as those wanting to support the foster parents they knew. It has actually surprised me how often it comes up in conversations with various people who simply want to know more. Either they are considering foster parenting or have close friends who are already fostering parenting. Just this morning, while talking with a friend about our art, she mentioned having a different friend who is a foster parent and is feeling very isolated. That led to me sharing with my friend some practical and helpful ideas—like the things included in this book—so she could reach out to that mom. Shortly after that, someone I only know through another friend, reached out to me on social media. We had a conversation online of her own adoption as a child and her desire to now adopt a child, along with the challenges that go with that.

When I returned home after walking with my friend on that Question and Answer day with Matt, I replayed the section of the live Q&A for Randy. I was hoping that Randy too would think it was a crazy idea. After all, I was a quilt artist, not an author! Randy calmly suggested we pray about it. That seemed reasonable and we agreed to pray about it for a few days. I admit I really just wanted to skip the whole crazy book idea. Over the next few days, we prayed and finally we agreed that it was time to share our experience with others in a book. So, here we are.

In sharing our story, I desire to guide you through some of the most common topics of foster parenting and adoption that will help you along your own foster parent journey. Because each story is true, I have changed the names and identifying details of the children, caseworkers, and others to maintain confidentiality.

The chapter "Drafting a Strong Professional Team" is key to setting yourself up for not only a successful placement but in the necessary relationships and meetings with others on your team who you will be involved with.

"Choosing a Private or a State Agency" compares our experience working with a private agency with the experience of a friend who first chose to work directly with the state agency.

"The Honeymoon Period" will prepare you for the neck-snapping switch you may experience as the sweet child you brought into your home begins to let out their strong emotions in unpleasant ways.

"Organization" offers a wide variety of methods I used to keep our home and myself organized. The extra organizational efforts allowed me to focus on family life and the children in our home, and created time for other activities.

"Boundaries Build Butterflies" is about the boundaries we set in our home and how the children maneuvered within them. It also has examples of how we proceeded when the child did not follow those boundaries.

The chapter "Teaching Life Skills" is full of practical ideas and ways that we offered each child opportunities to learn skills that would not only benefit them while in our home but would mold them for their life as an adult.

In the chapter "Self-Care Is Not Selfish," I share how we learned that it is vital to care for ourselves, mind and body, so we could continue our season of being foster parents. Related to that is the chapter "Everyone Needs a Break — Respite Care" where I offer ideas and tips that worked for us as we offered and received respite.

"Foster to Adopt" is our personal adoption journey, as well as stories of some of our friends who also chose to adopt after fostering.

Throughout the stories of the children who were in our home, I have woven the techniques I learned to better care for myself physically and emotionally, which resulted in the ability to better enjoy the process.

I believe that both husband and wife need to be committed to the calling of being a foster parent. I often have someone tell me that they would love to be a foster parent but their spouse is not for it. When they ask what I think, I tell them that I believe that the Lord calls both spouses although not always at the same time, as in my case. All children need parents who work together as a team toward the same goal. I learned that teamwork is even more critical when you are a foster parent. It is similar to couples wanting to have children by birth, both need to want children or there will always be a tension when issues arise. And issues *will* arise, whether your children are by birth or otherwise.

I wasn't prepared when all our friends and family were not as excited as we were about our choice to foster parent. Our time was often taken up with meetings, medical appointments, therapy and continuing foster parent classes to maintain our license. Sometimes, it's hard to maintain relationships when so much time is focused on caring for another's child. Many well-meaning friends and acquaintances shared horror stories about foster parenting, out of concern for us. That's why I believe it was vital that I knew we had been called to this role as foster parents for a season. Young lives had the opportunity to be forever changed for the good whether they expressed their appreciation or not—and most did not. It was still worth it.

I am thankful for the input I have to offer you through this book as you navigate your foster or adoptive parenting adventure. Or maybe your desire is to help a family member or friend who is seeking to navigate it. Either way, know that I am praying for you to be the best foster parent you can be and I hope you will one day also share your journey with others as well. Let's get started!

# CHAPTER ONE

# DRAFTING A STRONG PROFESSIONAL TEAM

Sadly, when children would come into our home, many had not visited a doctor, dentist, or had their eyes examined in quite a while. At times, immunizations were behind, cavities needed filling, and glasses prescribed. I imagine going to a medical appointment was not the child's favorite outing even before coming into our home. Adding to the mix was usually a new medical provider for the child as they moved to our home. I learned over time that when Randy and I had previous experience with a particular medical professional the appointments went much smoother for us and for the child too.

So, what do I mean by drafting a strong professional team? I mean that choosing a team of doctors, a dentist, therapist, and other professionals to work with your child is key to a successful foster care placement and possible adoption. There were so many unknowns with the children that came into our home and we found it best to have trusted professionals in place that we already knew and had experience with. If you don't already have these professionals in place, it is well worth the effort and time to ask trusted friends and or family for references. It's never too early to begin asking for references to build your professional team. Follow those recommendations with an internet search, a phone call, email, or office visit to get valuable insight into which professionals will work best with your family. Save yourself the aggravation by working with professionals who mirror your values. We met with a few therapists for a consultation in advance since we knew that working collaboratively with them would be a vital part of the therapy process. Not all trained therapists are specifically trained to help children who have had adverse childhood experiences (ACEs), resulting in trauma both before and during their time in the foster care system. I would suggest that you seek out a therapist with a good track record and experience with children who have childhood trauma as part of their past and who value and respect you as foster parents.

Even if a child is already seeing a therapist, you may request that the child coming into your home change to your family therapist. If the team is not in favor of this, you may want to decline the placement into our home. You have what's called "client choice," if there is an indication that this child will not work out well in your home. We found that a therapist who is a poor fit for you and the child can cause more trauma for the child. The therapist particularly needs to be in sync with your family values, ideologies, beliefs, and goals.

Foster parents do have the right to choose a professional team for the children who will be in their home. And you have the right to say "no" to the placement of a child if the professional team is not one that will work well with your family as a whole.

I found it helpful to have a colored folder to keep forms and official letters in one place that I would need when going to medical type visits. Especially when we had more than one child in our home, I made sure the folders were different colors to make taking the correct folder for the child with me simpler. Often, I let the child choose their favorite color for their folder. In that folder, I kept the copy of the child's current Medicaid card and immunization records. I also kept a copy of the order of custody paper from the social services office stating that Randy and I were indeed the foster parents of that particular child and had authority to sign school or church activity wavers as well as seek medical help for them. Yes, doctor and dentist offices will ask to see that form when you first go for a visit. Never mind how I know that. Each child's folder additionally housed a copy of the child's report card until the next home visit with the caseworker who would collect it. After a child would leave our home, I would destroy all the confidential papers and information.

Donovan was in first grade when he can to stay with us and we needed to take him for a well visit with a doctor in my area since he had moved from another county. The well visit was to establish a baseline in Donovan's health and to give him the opportunity to meet the doctor. My own biological children had passed the pediatrician stage so I no longer had current information on local pediatricians. The well visit for Donovan had to happen shortly after he came into our home, as he would be attending a new school. The Department of Social Service (DSS) caseworker, Mr. John, told me to take him to a specific large group practice. I did not have any experience with that office. I didn't realize it at the time, but I could have chosen a different practice for Donovan. *Client choice.* Not all medical practices accept Medicaid, the insurance Donovan had, so that was a factor as well. Medicaid was a new experience for us and we weren't familiar with Medicaid guidelines and requirements.

We learned that not all DSS caseworkers would let you know that you had *client choice*. Caseworkers are usually already overwhelmed by their caseloads and sometimes it is quicker for them to recommend someone they already know. Remember— the foster parent can choose which medical offices to work with.

I'm a big advocate for children being in school for the whole school day. Most children who came into our home were behind in school to some degree. Some were years behind. I knew they needed after-school appointments that didn't disrupt their learning. While I understand that pulling some kids out of school for appointments is fine, we felt this was not a good option for Donovan. He was already significantly behind. So, when I was given a pediatric appointment for Donovan during the school day, I insisted on something after school.

Donovan did well in the waiting room as he read aloud to me from one of his school books. He tensed up though when the nurse called him by his full name and referred to me as Mrs. and his last name. Although it was an innocent mistake, I'm guessing Donovan was already feeling weird about meeting a new doctor but he glanced at me as if to say, "She's *not* my mom." After that, I made it my habit to quickly introduce myself. I also would say that the child was "staying with us for a while" instead of calling them my "foster child." I never liked the "foster child" label; it seemed to make everyone uncomfortable. I prefer thinking of the young person as a child in the foster care system instead of a "foster child." No one ever questioned what I meant by, "They are staying with us for a while."

Weighing in was embarrassing for Donovan. He was overweight and now everyone would know. It was a very vulnerable situation for Donovan and I wasn't totally comfortable with it either. Moreover, this was not the child-friendly, caring office I had hoped for. Dr. Samuel came across as insensitive to Donovan's uncomfortableness Still, I had followed through on getting Donovan his wellness check and the medical form we had to return to our caseworker, Mr. John, was completed and signed. The experience had left me feeling awkward. I am sure Donovan picked up on that as well.

Simple things like smiling at Donovan and talking more *with* him and not *about* him like he wasn't in the room would have made the atmosphere much more child friendly.

Looking back, had I known I could have chosen, I would have sought out an appointment with our long-time family physician and checked to see if he took Medicaid.

Thankfully, by the time it came to Donovan's need to see a dentist, I had learned that I could choose my preferred provider. I contacted several friends for recommendations and found that there was a wonderful children's dental practice nearby that accepted Medicaid, since our family dentist did not. Dr. Charles was highly recommended by everyone who had experience with him. His office was excellent in every way and although Donovan went into that appointment wide-eyed, it was a good experience for him. The dental hygienist was cheerful, engaging Donovan right away and had him laughing by the time she was checking his weight, height, and temperature. Interestingly, the dentist office preformed all those checks on Donovan in case he required any medicines, which are generally prescribed based on height, weight and age. Dr. Charles was just as upbeat and I was impressed by the friendliness and respect Donovan was shown by everyone in the office. The examination room was open and held four dental examination tables and all the young patients seemed at ease. There was a genuine mutual respect among the staff. And even though the examination revealed cavities, Donovan seemed good with returning to this office for the fillings since it had been such a positive experience. I believe because Donovan knew I had already checked out and trusted this dentist, he had a positive experience.

It was a blessing that our family eye doctor took Medicaid and Donovan had a good experience there as well. I'm not sure Donovan had ever had his eyes checked by a professional before then. We were all surprised that he not only needed glasses but a strong prescription at that. I was amazed that Donovan had been able to begin reading so well and succeed in his classroom with such poor eyesight. He happily chose some stylish frames and actually looked forward to wearing glasses. Being able to see better was exciting for him. I was so thankful since not all the children who lived with us and had glasses would wear them.

Over time, as Donovan walked with me every day after school, played in the yard, ate healthy homemade meals instead of processed food, his weight lowered to normal for his size. He brushed his teeth regularly avoiding more cavities. He learned to try new fruits and vegetables, enjoyed being my sous chef, and gained confidence overall. And while he lived in our home, Donovan rarely got sick, making doctor visits rare.

I have no idea how many different doctors and dentist's offices Donovan had been in before our home or after he moved away. Realizing that the number would probably grow when he was moved to another home was sad. I maintained connections with the medical offices that worked for our family, keeping our strong team in place for future children. It made such a difference to have a team that worked together well so the medical issues could be addressed collaboratively.

Therapists fall into the medical appointment category, although it is more of a personal appointment for the foster parent as well. When twelve-year-old Sasha came to stay at our home we were told that it would be a very temporary placement as her parents were working to regain custody—three or four months, tops. Maybe for that reason or because the DSS caseworker, Mrs. Susan, was adamant about Sasha starting to work with a particular therapist that she was familiar with, we didn't push the issue. I knew several great therapists in the area and had never heard of this particular one, Dr. Chang. At the time, it seemed an unnecessary skirmish. Sasha was already moving from another city an hour away from her current therapist. Choosing to defer on that one decision wreaked havoc in our home. Up until that time, Randy and I had made the choice on the therapist for the children in our home. We had two different therapists, a male, Dr. Jones, and a female, Mrs. Miller that we preferred and who lined up with our family values. They each also had previous experience with children within the foster care system, adopted children, and children who had experienced trauma.

Time revealed that Sasha's parents were not actually meeting the requirements to regain custody as they reported they were doing. The three to four months Sasha was supposed to be with us turned into a couple of years. It was a hard time for Sasha and us to continue to live in a limbo state. Sasha's greatest desire was to return home and live with her parents regardless of the things that had happened before entering the foster care system. We had fallen in love with Sasha and talked about adopting her should the opportunity become available and Sasha began to talk about a future living with us, as well.

Meanwhile, the therapist, Dr. Chang, wasn't a good fit for Randy or me. Our values were very different and pleasing Sasha seemed to be Dr. Chang's main objective. At home, Sasha was making great progress learning boundaries, life skills, working together, and her school grades were improving. Therapy appointments were twice a month and scheduled for one hour; but consistently ran over since Dr. Chang would talk with me for a few minutes before talking with Sasha to see how Sasha was progressing. Or so I thought.

Sasha had wanted to participate in an after-school sporting team and Randy and I agreed that it might be a good thing for her. What we learned a few days into the practices when I went early to the practice to see how Sasha was doing was unsettling. Sasha wasn't at the practice that day and I learned Sasha wasn't always showing up for practice but was going elsewhere on campus with friends. When her lying about where she was came up in therapy, Dr. Chang suggested to me that we were too strict in our home and that Sasha needed more freedoms than she had proved to us was good for her. Sasha had also asked to participate in the youth group at our church and talked about how much she liked the youth director and the other students there. Yet, Dr. Chang suggested we were *making* her go. There were several more discrepancies and we realized that Sasha was doing and saying one thing at home and telling Dr. Chang another during her appointments. I asked numerous times for Dr. Chang, Sasha, and me to meet together but he continued to say that Sasha wasn't ready for that. It became more apparent that there was an unhealthy communication cycle occurring with Dr. Chang, Randy and me. We even contacted our caseworker, Mr. John, more than once to request a different therapist but were told again and again that it was not an option. Because we thought we were on a path to one day adopt Sasha, we kept thinking that we could wait this out and then choose our own therapist. It was suggested but never stated outright that Mr. John would request to move Sasha to a different home before considering changing her therapist. That kept us off balance and left us feeling disrespected.

I learned about the term "triangulation" from Dr. Henry Cloud, psychologist and bestselling author of the book *Boundaries*. He writes, "Triangulation occurs when person A tells a secret to person B, who then tells person C about it. Triangulation is a form of gossip and betrays a confidence. They may be pitting one person against another in a repetitive pattern from childhood."

When I suggested to Dr. Chang that I felt Sasha was using triangulation to use Dr. Chang to manipulate Randy and me to get her way in things, he dismissed the idea. Sasha's appointments became weekly and the time Dr. Chang talked with me in the beginning minutes seemed to be gathering information to use against Randy and me. My opinion and observations did not appear to be valued and I began to feel less and less a part of the team.

It was so frustrating not having clear communication among everyone and having the areas that were helping Sasha heal and grow be scrutinized and criticized. I knew we were doing a good job parenting Sasha and having our insights rejected left me feeling angry. Sasha grew more and more untruthful.

Each individual family has the right to decide if a child, foster or biological, shows responsibility for having a smartphone. This difficult decision is not limited to children being fostered. I know of many families of high school students who prefer that their children not have a smartphone at all. One family we know limits their teen's smartphone use to weekends only. Even with applications to help protect children on phones, we all know that kids are often able to figure a way around most smart phone and internet restrictions.

Against our better judgement, we allowed Sasha and Dr. Chang to convince us that Sasha "needed" a smartphone of her own as a freshman in high school. We had Sasha draw up a contract of sorts of guidelines that she felt would be fair and that we could all agree to.

Surprisingly, Sasha wrote up an excellent agreement including things we had not even considered. I suspected

Dr. Chang helped her with it. Some of her guidelines included a requirement that others be present in the room with her when she used the phone at home and that she leave the phone in the kitchen when she went into her room for the evening. Sasha included that she would pay for the phone herself knowing that this was something we would require. Sasha did a bit of babysitting for families at church and helped a neighbor with their small business at their home, but we were concerned that she would struggle to earn enough money to pay her monthly phone charges. Sasha also included in the agreement that her phone would be taken away for a period of time by Randy or me if she was using it inappropriately or as a consequence of negative behavior.

As we anticipated, the smartphone became a wedge between Sasha and us as she did not keep up her part of her written agreement. So many things became an arena for conflict with Sasha, Randy and me, like holding Sasha accountable for her lying and expecting her to be where she said she would be. Yet Dr. Chang continued to defend her. I began dreading the therapy afternoons more and more and found my stomach upset then as well. Randy and I grew more perplexed as to why Dr. Chang was believing the untruths from Sasha.

Without Chang's support for Randy and me, chaos and distance were generated among the adults. Instead of working together as a strong team for Sasha's benefit the focus became that Randy and me were now bad parents. Those lies began to deceptively creep into my heart.

Randy and I continued to pray for truth to be revealed and yet, as this situation continued to spiral down, I found myself losing sleep and feeling less hope that resolution was possible.

I remember Dr. Chang commenting once a few weeks prior that we were just paid parents. I felt hurt and misunderstood since we truly loved every child that entered our home even for a weekend. The more I thought back to that comment, the angrier I felt to have my character and motives assaulted. We always felt that each child deserved the best we had to offer as parents and loved them for who they were regardless of their behavior or prior circumstances.

Over time, it became evident that there would not be a resolution among the adults. I cried so many tears of disbelief and sadness over the unraveling of the hope to move forward in our relationship with Sasha. My stomach hurt most of the time and sleep was fitful. Randy and I kept asking the Lord for a breakthrough in this situation and yet it did not come. Finally, through much prayer, heart-wrenching tears, and disappointment, Randy and I chose to *give our notice* for Sasha. I'd never heard the phrase "give notice" for a child in the foster care system until our caseworker suggested that it might be an option for us in this situation. That made it sound like a job and we never considered foster parenting a job. Our decision gave Mr. John thirty days to find another home for Sasha. Our hearts were broken. Even writing about it still brings emotional tears. What a sad ending to a potentially successful adoption for a child's life by a family that loved them.

I didn't realize it then, but one negative comment after another from Sasha and Dr. Chang and lack of support from them and Mr. John about us as parents and foster parents took root in my heart. Each lie told about me caused me to question who I was as an experienced and loving mom and as a person. Comments like *being old fashioned, too strict, not letting the child be free, being critical, just fostering for the money, not very wise* tore my heart apart. I came to realized that these untruths were coming from a couple of professional people who didn't seem to know me well and who seemed to choose to put me down. As I have talked with other foster and adoptive moms over time, I continue to hear the same story. They too allow the hurtful comments or lack of support of others to cause them to question their ability as a mom. And considering many children in the foster care system are angry with not being with their birth parents, they too often add to the sinking feeling of being devalued in the foster mom role.

When I began examining the lies that I had allowed to influence my heart, I slowly got back to believing truth about myself. I encourage moms I talk with now to do the same. What we believe about ourselves is critical to remaining healthy, not just for our own benefit but also for the children who come through our home.

When nine-year-old Jamal came to live with us, he had been in the foster care system for over six years.

Being in the system so long, he had learned to manipulate and *work* the system to what he thought was his benefit. Jamal was excellent at what we called "flying under the radar." Jamal had learned to "yes ma'am" and "no sir," as his way around most situations and to avoid having to acknowledge his own pain. Jamal wasn't the first child we had had that was great at avoiding issues but certainly one of the cleverest and most resourceful. I set up an appointment for Jamal with our chosen trusted male therapist, Dr. Jones, whom we had known for many years. The fact that Dr. Jones knew Randy and me so well was an asset and saved a lot of time and energy during sessions. When he suspected that Jamal wasn't being truthful about something that had happened in our home, Dr. Jones would question it with Jamal alone and then ask me about it at the end of the session with Jamal still present. Jamal quickly learned that the adults were on the same team and that his manipulation wasn't working to divide us. The strength of us being a team allowed Dr. Jones to spend the therapy time truly dealing with Jamal's hurt heart from his past and not focus on fabricated drama. That also gave Dr. Jones the freedom to help Randy and me learn new ways of helping Jamal heal as well. It's easy to feel sorry for a child with all they have been through but there's a difference between that and helping them heal. Dr. Jones encouraged Randy and me to keep perspective and to continue having safe boundaries with Jamal without getting sucked into his "poor me" attitude. Dr. Jones was a cheerleader for Randy and me as well, often reminding us of the things we were doing well that were helping Jamal heal.

Although many deep, deep wounds were revealed in Jamal's heart, he was finally looking at them which, although painful, were for his good. It was hard to hear some of the trauma details of Jamal's past and embarrassing for him as well. The energy he'd used to hide pain was now being used to grieve. Many days it was not pretty, yet exposing the truth gave Jamal the opportunity to heal and move forward. I understood that it would be up to Jamal to continue to heal using the new therapeutic tools he was gaining. Our part was offering him a quality therapist as part of a strong team.

Not all the professionals who worked with the children in our home were good matches. We did our best to work with everyone involved and at times chose to either revise our team or, as a last resort, to ask for the child to be moved to another home. Neither was fun but having a strong professional team was a valuable key to keeping our home a safe and peaceful environment.

# CHAPTER TWO

# CHOOSING A PRIVATE OR A STATE AGENCY

The ultimate goal of private and state agencies is the welfare of the child and the foster family. Both private and state agencies can arrange respite for their foster families. Usually each agency, whether private or state, draws from the pool of foster parents within their own agency. In general, in a private foster care agency, the caseworkers each have a smaller caseload than those of state foster care agencies. I learned that a child in the foster care system is in the legal custody of that state, and the state's first priority is the child.

When we began our journey into foster parenting neither of us were aware of the names of any private agencies that worked with foster parents nor were we familiar with how the agencies operated. We also had not had any personal experience with the state foster parent agency.

We really didn't know where or how to start the process of finding out if there were children that needed a home after Hurricane Katrina. Later into our journey, we met couples who liked working directly with the state foster care agency. I found it interesting that there were differences between how counties operate even within the same state. There was not a one size fits all in our state.

We met many couples who preferred a private foster care agency. There is no charge for using a private agency rather than a state agency for fostering children, so that is not a factor.

I always encourage parents to seek out information from others or on the internet for their particular area and state before choosing which will work best for their family.

Interestingly, it never occurred to me to check first with the state foster care agency when seeking information about children who might need a home after the hurricane disaster. If we were to choose to become foster parents again, we would again choose a private agency that best aligned with our family values because we appreciated the additional support for us as parents.

Once we decided to explore adoption, I began by calling Red Cross and other disaster relief type agencies that I *was* familiar with. Several years earlier, we had housed unwed, pregnant mothers so I also called that agency as well knowing that they sometimes assisted in child adoptions. I called various organizations for several days. It seemed like no one knew the information I wanted or who to direct me to. I eventually found and contacted a couple private foster care agencies. When I called them, I got the impression that I was talking to sales representatives instead of people who were actually listening and was trying to answer my question. I felt discouraged and more confused than when I had started. I deleted them from my list of possible options.

The process left me frustrated and irritated and I began to have doubts about whether we heard the Lord calling us to adopt after all.

After what felt like too many dead ends, one day I prayed, "Lord, You'll just have to have them call me because I don't know who else to call." Imagine my surprise when the very next day, Mr. Reid, the director of a neighboring county Christian children's group home, called me. Randy and I were trained volunteer financial coaches with a national Christian organization who gave Mr. Reid our names and contact information. Mr. Reid explained that he was working with some parents who were not fulfilling their financial obligation for their three children who lived in the group home. This couple, Mr. and Mrs. Hudson, was giving Mr. Reid conflicting information about their finances and were not doing the things required to regain custody of their children. Mr. Reid hoped that we could offer more clarity into their situation by meeting with them. After several minutes of describing their circumstances, Mr. Reid asked if we would be willing to have them contact us and meet. We had never met with a couple in this type of situation and, to be honest, I wasn't sure I wanted to be part of the equation. It would be great if Randy and I could help them but I didn't get the impression from Mr. Reid that the Hudsons actually wanted help. Reluctantly, I agreed. Mr. Reid could pass along our phone number so the Hudsons could call us and set up a meeting.

As I hung up the telephone, I sensed the Lord say, "That was THE call you were asking for." What? That seemed like a crazy answer to my prayer.

Sheepishly, I called Mr. Reid right back and told him my story of endless days seeking information about children needing to be adopted in the aftermath of Hurricane Katrina. I added that his call may have been the answer to my prayer although I couldn't image how. Mr. Reid asked if we wanted to adopt the Hudson's children since it appeared they might soon need a home. I was stunned and said I didn't know what I wanted but that I just knew his call was *the call* I had asked the Lord for. He started laughing and explained that my call wasn't the first of that type he had received. Instead, he offered to connect us with his friend Wade who was a caseworker with a private foster care agency. They were longtime friends and he felt Wade would be able to help me. Finally, someone who might answer our question about children in need of a home after the disaster.

It wasn't like we were purposefully seeking a private foster care agency to represent us. Or any type of agency for that matter. We were simply seeking options that we hoped might point us in the direction toward kids who may need a family in the aftermath of the hurricane. Why had it all been so complicated?

I contacted Wade and set up a time for Randy and me to meet with him, just to get some information. We liked Wade right away as our values of family and life in general seemed to line up well with him personally. As Wade talked, we realized that the private foster care agency he represented might be a good fit for us if we chose to go ahead with any of this. Wade also helped us understand that the next logical step in our journey to seek out a child who needed to be adopted might be for us to first become trained as foster parents. Children in need of a home aren't just given over to a family without the supervision of the state's foster care system. That made sense although I hadn't planned on becoming a foster parent. Yet, we knew we were serious about the possibility of taking in a child. So, we chose to be trained by the private foster care agency that Wade represented and Wade actually became our first case manager.

Interestingly, we never met with Mr. and Mrs. Hudson from the group home to help clarify issues with their finances. They never came for any of their scheduled appointments with us.

In our state, the foster care agency is called the Department of Social Services (DSS). I've learned that states vary in what they call the state foster care agencies. Some states call it the Department of Child Services (DCS), Department of Children and Families (DCF),

Child Protective Services (CPS), etc. I find it a little confusing.

Because Randy and I went directly to a private agency, I didn't know the differences between state and private agencies at that time. I did know that both state and private agencies assigned each family a caseworker as the liaison between the agency and the family. I also knew that they both worked for the welfare of the child. I thought every foster parent family received the support for them as parents like we did from our private agency. As we met more foster parents, I realized that was not true for many families that worked directly with the state agency. I often heard other foster moms express their irritation with a sense of not being listened to by their caseworker. Often their caseworker had so many cases, it was difficult for them to give the time that the foster moms felt they needed. Those type of conversations made me appreciate my caseworkers more and value the support they offered.

I contacted my friend Lisa to ask permission to share her and Leo's story of working with a state agency. At one time, when Lisa and I were both foster moms, we talked and connected a lot, but we have lost touch since then. Because I am familiar with Leo and Lisa's story, I hesitated to contact her. I suspected it would be difficult to ask Lisa questions I was sure would bring up heartbreaking memories. I know it is hard for me when people ask tough questions about our foster care season. My desire to share the whole story and not just the nice and neat parts that I'd prefer to tell is important to me and that is why I am doing this. And I was pretty sure Lisa would feel the same way when I told her I was writing a book.

For me, writing this book has brought back many memories, not all of them good. While much of my foster parenting season was joyful and fun, some experiences I'd rather forget. While I have healed much of the pain in my heart, I'm not finished yet. Being a foster parent and particularly a foster mom potentially opens you up for a lot of criticism from the children, caseworkers, birth parents, and friends. And family. And because I know how the memories can still sting, I didn't want to open up wounds in my friend Lisa. Thankfully, because Lisa and I had built a trusting relationship, she agreed to set up a time to talk with me.

Randy and I met Leo and Lisa at church. Actually, Leo and I had been part of a mission trip team that traveled to Nicaragua for ten days after the devastation of Hurricane Mitch in 1998. Leo and Lisa already had two boys from birth, Michael and Mason, when they decided that they wanted to adopt a little girl. They went through the process of taking the necessary classes, going through the home study that assured their home was a safe place, background checks, and all the paperwork to become licensed through the state agency in our county. I was impressed that in the meantime, Lisa, being quite internet savvy, located and became involved in an online nationwide support group for adoptive parents. Randy and I weren't even considering being foster parents at that time, so it was all new to us.

Being new to the foster care system herself, Lisa did not know that their foster care license was for our state only. It was through the online support group that she learned about three-year-old Pam who only spoke about ten words of English and about ten words of Spanish. Pam had already been adopted from Russia into a Latino family but the placement was not working out. Pam had been made available for a second-chance adoption into another family, something I'd never heard of. Leo and Lisa learned more about Pam and fell in love with her. Lisa began gathering information on how they could adopt Pam. Lisa learned about the Interstate Compact of the Placement of Children (ICPC), which is a contract that allows states that are members to work together for the child's welfare and protection across state lines. So, Leo and Lisa used an agency in another state for the interstate compact as per the law—but only for paperwork. All the paperwork was filed though each state's capitol office, meaning their local county section of the state agency was not involved. Leo and Lisa were thrilled that Pam was now legally their adopted daughter. There was no ongoing support offered to them from either state in their adoption, so Lisa continued with her online adoption support group.

At that time, Randy and I and a few other couples met at Leo and Lisa's home for a weekly small group. We were all so excited when we finally got to meet Pam one Wednesday night. With her short blond hair and cute face, she shyly hid a bit behind Lisa. This was before Randy and I began our foster parent journey and we found it all intriguing. We were so thrilled for Leo and Lisa and their young growing family.

Adjusting to their recent adoption of Pam, Leo and Lisa didn't have other children from the foster care system in their home for several months. I lost touch with Lisa a bit during this time as she was busy helping Pam acclimate to their family.

Ms. June was their foster care worker with the state agency in our county and she was only required to have a quarterly home visit with Leo and Lisa. Lisa and Ms. June did build a relationship during that time and Lisa felt supported by her, calling Ms. June when needed. Lisa believed that Ms. June showed genuine understanding without judgment.

After several months, Pam was adjusting nicely to being a part of Leo, Lisa, Michael, and Mason's family and home. Leo and Lisa felt it was time to begin having additional children from the foster care system into their home. Ms. June placed Alex and Emily into their home. Alex and Emily were siblings and they had two other siblings living in a different foster care home. All four of the siblings were what is called a *sibling set* and are kept together if at all possible.

Alex and Emily appeared to be a good fit for Leo and Lisa's home so they were considering adopting them and possibly the other two siblings as well. I thought Leo and Lisa were very brave to not only adopt Pam but to be considering adopting a sibling set of four too! OK, maybe

I really thought they were a bit crazy but I never said that out loud. Leo and Lisa were great parents and their home had plenty of bedrooms, but that would make a total of seven children. At that time, it was permissible to adopt several children, although our state has now limited the number.

In the middle of Leo and Lisa looking at adopting the sibling set of four children, Ms. June went out on maternity leave and the situation went into chaos. Their new caseworker, Mrs. Sue, blamed Leo and Lisa for the confusion and began speaking badly about them as foster parents. Leo and Lisa no longer felt represented or understood and could not get the answers they needed to move forward with the adoptions. Things got worse. Alex and Emily were removed from their home leaving Leo and Lisa confused, hurt, and frustrated. I wasn't living this, but it seemed that if the state had a safe and caring home with great parents who loved this sibling set of four and were willing to adopt them, why not work to make that happen? Leo and Lisa were devastated. I would have been too.

We've had children removed from our home due to lies told about us, which is something I never expected when we became foster parents. When the situation turns sideways, it can cause you to question yourself as a parent and lose confidence in the foster care system that is more broken than I first realized.

I knew Leo and Lisa wanted only to help children have a secure and loving home. I would say that most foster parents we encountered had a heart for the welfare of the child. That situation led Leo and Lisa to seek out and find a private foster care agency that aligned with their family goals and values and gave them the additional support they needed as foster parents.

I'd like to say Leo and Lisa had smooth sailing going forward but that isn't true. What they did have was the support that they needed and desired. Later, Leo and Lisa adopted Emma, Olivia, and Logan, all from different families. All of the children Leo and Lisa had by birth and adopted are now grown and living on their own. Leo and Lisa moved away from our area a while ago, trading their very large home for a smaller one that fits their current needs as empty nesters.

It was good albeit hard to talk with Lisa to refresh my memory of their story. I enjoyed catching up but it was also hard for Lisa to retell this part of her story. I can appreciate that. I got choked up as I was listening to her, as it triggered hurtful places in my heart as well. We also talked how the passage of time and deliberately working to heal our hearts, we had each come out stronger as women and with stronger marriages. We talked of how we had done our best to offer love and healing to each child who came into our home with great trauma, regardless of whether the child embraced that. We had given each child our all and felt good about doing so.

Before hanging up, I asked Lisa what she would want readers to take away from her experience. Lisa said, "Find support online or otherwise. Look at the whole picture with older kids, not just the pretty side. Be aware that what you see now is not always what you will get when the kids are teens or adults. Parents must work to be a strong team, not divided and conquered. It's the only way to do it."

I totally agree.

I had never considered when we began our foster parenting journey that there were so many sibling sets in the foster care system. Since that time, I've come to understand that even though it may seem best to keep sibling sets together, that is not always the best choice for the children or the foster parent family. We found it a hard choice to make knowing a child who would be placed in our home had siblings that we were not going to foster as well. Sometimes it was a physical space issue since each child needs to have their own bed and sometimes a separate bedroom depending on their situation. Our home had two available bedrooms. Other times, it was based on our ability to give the needed care for more than one child at a time. At times, the child placed in our home may not have been safe living in the same home with their sibling. Sometimes one sibling needed a higher level of care than the one that was in our home. There are so many variables. Randy and I had to do what was best for our family at that time and only foster the children that were a good fit for us. Randy and I always made sure we prayed about this and were on the same page before accepting the placement of any child into our home. Not that that made the decision an easy one, but one we agreed on from the beginning.

Not all private agencies are the same. Once, I talked with a man at an agency who proudly stated that his agency paid better than any other agency in the area. I was annoyed that there seemed to be a competition to get new foster parents. I didn't call him back. I found out later that private foster care agencies do actually vary in payments to the foster parents although that was not our primary reason for choosing an agency or not.

One of my highest requirements was for our Christian beliefs to be honored. Back when I was seeking general information, someone mentioned to me that it would be best that we not talk about our Christian values. I later discovered that this was not true. It did cause me to begin mentioning that we were Christians when I would contact an agency and ask if that would be an issue. Most of those I talked with at the private agencies waffled when they answered, helping me to eliminate them from consideration. The agency that we chose to work with was a Christian private agency that said they were really glad we were Christians.

One of the positives of working with a private agency—especially one that aligns with your family values—is that you have a caseworker who will advocate for you as a foster parent. We found that having that extra advocate was often helpful during our foster care season. Not only did our caseworkers help us navigate the foster parenting world of meetings, classes, and protocols, but they helped us when issues arose. Over time, situations would change within our private agency and we would get a different caseworker. As we built relationships with each one, it was evident that they cared about Randy and I as foster parents as well as the children they placed within our home.

We saw that there can be a lot of turnover in caseworker positions in both private and state foster care agencies for various reasons. Often caseworkers work long hours and their personal family needs may change causing them to change positions within the agency or to move to a different job all together. Because Randy and I chose to stay in the foster care system for twelve years, we had about nine or ten different caseworkers within our same private foster care agency. Even with numerous caseworkers, our agency overall did a great job in supporting Randy and I as foster parents as well as the children that were placed within our home. One particular story comes to mind when I think of how I appreciated being supported by our caseworker in our private agency.

Four-year-old Grady and his ten-year-old sister Daisy came to stay in our home from another county on a wintery day. They were sad to be going anywhere except back to their birth parent's home. It always hurt my heart to see children want what they are familiar with even though it is not good for them. In our state, when a child is placed in the foster care system they remain as part of their home county and are assigned a caseworker within the state agency from that county. No matter where the children are moved to, they continue to remain under the authority of that county and have a caseworker from there. Grady and Daisy's caseworker from the state agency in that different county was Mrs. Barnes.

Grady and Daisy's mom still had limited visitation rights, which was not something we were used to. Most of the children who came through our home did not have parents that were involved in their lives. That is hard on the child but it also could be a blessing if the parent was not a good influence on them. Either way, it was hard to witness.

Grady and Daisy's mom contacted Mrs. Barnes requesting weekly parent visits and also weekly meetings with me to co-parent. I was not familiar with how co-parenting worked within the foster care system. I contacted our caseworker, Mrs. Nora, to get more information. She told me that sometimes it is helpful to get the birth parent and the foster parent together away from the children and discuss things that would be helpful for the children. Mrs. Nora mentioned that co-parenting meetings could be an asset in helping the children adjust to the foster home, allowing the birth parents to know everyday things about their children and have input into their lives. The meetings can also offer helpful information about the children that make living in the foster home easier.

I admit I was skeptical since I had already been verbally chewed out by Grady and Daisy's mom the first time we met. I was delivering the children to our agency's office for their first parent visit after they had come to live in our home. I had forgotten a paper in my car and went to get it quickly before their mom arrived at her appointed parent visit time. Grady and Daisy's mom came to the appointment very early. As I was coming back into the building, she saw me in the hallway and realized I was the foster mom where her children lived. She loudly proclaimed that she was a great mom and her children were "stolen" from her. She went on to tell me that I would never be any kind of mom to them. She also let me know that she would be fighting for her children at every turn so I should be on my guard. I relayed that encounter to Mrs. Nora and expressed my concern about any co-parenting meetings. Mrs. Nora advocated on my behalf to Mrs. Barnes but the co-parenting meetings were approved and I was required to attend.

At the first co-parenting meeting, Grady and Daisy's DSS worker Mrs. Barnes was there to oversee and supervise the meeting. The mom spent most of the allotted hour telling me how I could and should cater to her children's wishes, desires, and demands. She objected to my cooking, my choice of laundry detergent, our home guidelines, where we lived, and on and on.

The birth mom also used this meeting to verbally attack me as a person and as a parent.

For some reason, Mrs. Barnes from the state agency, who was clearly aware of what was happening, did not offer any support on my behalf. I wasn't sure what to say. I was taken off guard as I expected this meeting to be a give and take for the benefit of the children. I had taken time to drive to the agency office, in an attempt to better parent Grady and Daisy and was instead being criticized by someone who didn't even know me or had ever been to my home. And why wasn't Mrs. Barnes controlling this meeting? This was not OK. I was puzzled, hurt, and angry. This was not co-parenting—this was bullying and harassment.

I dreaded the next co-parenting meeting and hoped Mrs. Nora would be supervising this time. Instead, Mrs. Barnes was there and the same scenario was repeated. I was furious. Randy and I talked about what we needed to do next because this was obviously not working. We already greatly cared for Grady and Daisy even though they had only been with us for a few weeks. They were starting to settle in at school and in our home. Still the co-parenting meetings without support could not continue.

I contacted Mrs. Nora and requested a separate meeting with her. Mrs. Nora came out to our home and I met with her in her car so the children could not hear what I had to say. My heart was pounding as I talked with her about what was happening during the so-called co-parenting meetings. I also told Mrs. Nora that I would not be part of this type of meeting any longer since I was not receiving the support I needed and deserved. I further told Mrs. Nora that having to say all this was heart wrenching, since I realized this could mean that Grady and Daisy would possibly be moved from our home. We did not want the children to have to be moved again. That was not what we wanted but if these abusive co-parenting meetings continued to be required of me, the children would need to be moved.

How had it come to this? We were great foster parents and knew our home was a safe and potentially healing place for the children. Still, I needed to set a boundary and not continue to endure the weekly negative barrage from the birth mom. I also knew this put Mrs. Nora in a tough spot, needing to confront Mrs. Barnes and possibly pulling Grady and Daisy from our home. Thankfully, Mrs. Nora met with Mrs. Barnes and it was agreed that the co-parenting meetings would cease. There was also a change in the timing for when I dropped Grady and Daisy off for visits with their birth mom. She was no longer able to come early to the meetings, giving me plenty of time to leave before she arrived.

I appreciated having Mrs. Nora as an advocate in that situation. Things could have turned out so differently otherwise. I never learned why Mrs. Barnes was silent during those meetings and allowed the verbal abuse I received. I suspected she was afraid to cross the birth mom. Whatever her reason, it made me extra appreciative of the support I did receive from Mrs. Nora.

With our private agency, we experienced the benefit of the teamwork and network of support within the agency itself. Our agency had regular meetings between supervisors and caseworkers to get updates on each case and family as well as brain storming solutions for problems. In other words, we not only received the benefit of our particular caseworker but indirect help from their co-workers and supervisors as well.

Since Randy and I were required to receive continuing training hours to keep our foster care license up to date, it was helpful that our agency hosted these training sessions. That helped us obtain our training hours gradually instead of cramming right before applying for a renewal of our license.

In my state, a foster parent license is good for two years, requiring twenty in-service training hours for a basic family care license for that time period. Everything from keeping up-to-date CPR and first aid certificates to topics specifically related to caring for the children was covered. Twenty training hours for a two-year period may not seem like a lot but it can be a challenge to manage along with the many other appointments and meetings that are necessary as a foster parent.

Randy and I were also trained as therapeutic foster parents, which requires an additional twenty in-service training hours in a two-year period. Therapeutic foster parents need the extra training to care for children who have been identified as needing more specialized care. We found that attending training sessions within our private agency not only offered us opportunity to get our necessary training hours but also to see and get to know other caseworkers and supervisors within our agency. That was valuable if our caseworker became sick or had a personal emergency and another worker within the private agency had to fill in. It also offered a time to meet with other foster parents within our private agency and get to know and encourage each other. Our agency usually offered a simple meal like pizza or subs and often childcare during the training sessions. This made attending the trainings easier for everyone. Additionally, we had opportunities to meet other children within the private agency's care. Since Randy and I often offered respite within our private agency, I appreciated that this time made us familiar with the children and they with us.

Over our foster parenting season, I met foster parents who enjoyed working directly with the state agency as well as others who enjoyed working with a private agency. We also knew foster parents who began working directly with the state agency and later sought out private agency as well. My experience and that of those I know may be totally different from those in your area. Remember, we started off with a private agency and did not have experience with state agencies. I always encourage others to seek out other foster care families and talk to them about their personal experiences before making that decision because each family is unique in its values and needs. I am so glad that Randy and I were together in the decision as we chose to go with a private agency. I believe the extra support we received made a big difference in our foster parent experience.

# CHAPTER THREE

# THE HONEYMOON PERIOD

I have found that we seem to all begin relationships letting others see the best of us. Even if we are having a bad day, we probably choose to smile and be pleasant. The same held true for the beginning of a relationship with a child entering our home from the foster care system. It's called a *honeymoon period*. As a general rule, Randy and I were on our best behavior, wanting the child to see us at our best. The child is usually also on their best behavior, wanting us to see the best of them. Without exception, every child who came into our home through foster care went through a honeymoon period where they were generally on their best behavior. The honeymoon period can last a few hours, a few days and, on rare occasions, a few months.

Most relationships go through stages of getting to know one another then becoming more comfortable as trust is offered and accepted. That's the best-case scenario.

You have probably experienced long-term relationships in which you might not see someone for a long time but you can pick up right where you left off. I've also experienced relationships that, for one reason or another, have drifted apart due to physical distance or schedules that make continuing the relationship prohibitive. And then, there's the relationship that you wonder really what it is. One of you gives a lot of energy to the relationship while the other doesn't reciprocate. Whatever type of relationship it is, it can be a challenge to build and maintain. All relationships take energy although care for children within foster care can be energy-intensive. The children are using so much of their energy learning a new home system, often a new school system, a new team of caseworkers, etc. It's exhausting, particularly when combined with the trauma the children bring with them. They might be holding it together on the outside, but are overwhelmed on the inside. Eventually, what's on the inside will come out. It's like a beach ball that is filled with air and held underwater. Ultimately, the beach ball will pop to the surface. And while foster care parents and the children in their home experience variances in relationships as well, it seems most of those relationships begin with a honeymoon period.

It helped me to remember that even though Randy and I were putting forth a lot of time and energy into building a relationship with each child, they might not have welcomed it. Keeping in mind that even though each child came into our home with some degree of trauma, they often wanted nothing more than to be home with their biological parents. It's like wanting a relationship with someone who resents the fact that you are even in their world.

If you are married, you might remember your honeymoon as a time right after the biggest positive decision you'd made in your entire life up until that moment. You had chosen to embark on a new and exciting adventure with someone you had chosen to love forever and build a life with. Life seemed perfect and you were going to conquer the world successfully together. Randy and I were married on a warm July Saturday night in south Florida surrounded by both of our large families and many friends. The church's air conditioning quit right before the service began and the sanctuary temperature climbed quickly. It didn't seem to matter to Randy and me because were really getting married! Even though we had planned for this day, it all seemed a bit surreal. Actually, I cried as I began to walk down the aisle. Not because I didn't want to marry Randy, but I knew this was a huge life change and the unknown seemed scary. We confidently said our "I dos" and were all smiles for the many, many, many photos. Whew, on to the party.

After the reception, we drove about an hour north and spent our first night as a married couple in a nearby hotel. We had made no reservations for anything for our honeymoon. We were on an adventure together and planned to take it one day at time. Our real destination was camping in the Blue Ridge Parkway campgrounds in the North Carolina Blue Ridge Mountains and on into Virginia in a pop-up camper that we borrowed from Randy's mom.

It didn't matter that we had no specific plans because I trusted Randy with my life and knew he loved me enough to take care of the details and navigate us well. Besides, he had an atlas. He's a detail guy and I'm a spur of the moment, "let's go." person. So, Randy drove and navigated while I had brought a sewing project along for the long ride. It was perfect. It never occurred to me that a new bride wouldn't take her most recent sewing project along on a long car ride, even if it was her honeymoon. We both were extra careful to be considerate with each other, even when we took our first trip to a grocery store. We compromised and choose one box of breakfast cereal that we could agree on to go with the fresh blackberries that we gleaned along our hikes. I felt I compromised the most since I don't like store-bought breakfast cereals. Still, we both chose to be flexible. It was just cereal after all. We enjoyed our camping honeymoon complete with horseback riding, canoeing down the Shenandoah River, and seeing a lot of wildlife on our hikes.

After ten days of seeing new sites, walking trails, and the like, we were tired and ready to drive back to Florida and get back to "normal." Back home, we cleaned and returned the pop-up camper. Randy went back to his front desk job and me to my waitress job at the resort hotel. Back to cooking dinner nightly, washing clothes in the apartment laundry room, paying the rent, lights, and all the duties of adult life. The honeymoon was over. Of course, that wasn't a bad thing as it actually was the beginning of a new normal that we would choose to make work for the forty-one years of our lives together at the time of this writing.

Knowing that each child came into our home not by their own choice, we chose to keep the honeymoon period as upbeat as possible. Days with home visits and medical and therapy appointments would begin soon enough. We offered an optimistic beginning to the relationship. In fact, Randy and I choose to be upbeat people most every day so it wasn't much of a challenge for us. Of course, those first honeymoon days seemed to go a bit better if the placement was a planned one where the child had met us before moving in rather than as an emergency placement where everything happened quickly without the opportunity to meet beforehand.

Randy and I have our quirks and preferences of how we like things to go as most everyone does. So, adding more people to the home mix brings readjustments for everyone. It was helpful to keep in mind that we were trained and more prepared for the transition than the child who came to us.

It was such a mix of emotions for me—excitement about giving a child a safe and loving home tinged with the sadness of knowing trauma had occurred in the child's life. *We* knew we were safe and loving, as did our agency and caseworker, but the child coming into our home didn't know that yet, not for sure. Trusting adults to be safe and loving and responsible had not always worked out well for the children who came into our home. The honeymoon period presented a relational mask that each child wore to navigate our home. We also recognized that since each child who came into our home had experienced trauma, there was most likely hurt and anger just below the surface. We all can put on a smile and press through new experiences for a while and then, like a marriage honeymoon, we return to normal.

Conner was eleven when he came to stay with us. On the outside, Conner had a fresh-from-the-barber-shop crew cut, loved to wear bright colors, and seemed willing to look at life with a thankful heart awaiting the next undertaking. His school records and testing showed he had a low IQ, which didn't offer much hope for him to excel in the scholastic arena. Everyone remarked that Conner was such a "happy kid." At first, he seemed a bit too happy especially around other people. Except me and Randy.

Conner's sixth grade math teacher, Mr. Olson, told me that Conner wasn't able to sit in class and that no matter how many times Mr. Olson explained the work, Conner couldn't learn it. Conner's other teachers expressed similar observations. At home Conner was becoming more comfortable and the honeymoon period was over. He had begun to express a great dislike for me. I came to realize that Conner's anger was really toward his birth mom who had left him at a very young age. And since his birth mom wasn't around to express his anger toward, Conner expressed it toward me. He would say hurtful things and stick out his tongue to me and when I called him on it in front of Randy, Conner acted as if I was picking on him. Conner lied often. He would argue the sky was green if given the opportunity, which we didn't after that first time. We thought Conner would adjust but his anger toward me increased, when no one else was looking of course. Usually at the end of Conner's therapy appointment, the therapist, Dr. Jones, would invite me into the office and would ask if I had anything I wanted to say about how things were going. On one particular day, I had picked up Conner right after school as I normally did but Conner's verbal venom was particularly strong. He told me he wanted me to die and that everything would be much better without me in the picture. Then it would be just him and Randy and everything would be perfect—without me. Conner even talked of how he hoped that Randy might marry his birth mom when I was gone. Of course, I was alarmed and creeped out but chose to wait to discuss it with Dr. Jones. When I mentioned that incidence, Conner acted greatly surprised and offended that I would accuse him of saying such a horrible thing. I was stunned. Conner's act was so believable that I begin to question if maybe I had misread the situation. I kept going back and forth between knowing what I had heard and watching Conner seem so convincing. Conner never did admit his cruel words and thankfully Dr. Jones, who was excellent and insightful, saw through Conner's act.

At the young age of eleven, Conner was already an expert at hiding behind his "I'm just a poor foster child" mask.

Sadly, his mask kept the trauma he had experienced hidden inside him, His mask postponed dealing with his past trauma and current behavior, and the healing that was offered to him.

It turned out that Conner was actually quite intelligent and had manipulated the school's testing system by pretending to not be smart so he wasn't expected to excel. He also liked receiving attention from the adults seeking to help him learn. It must have been exhausting for Conner to wear an emotional mask at school and then switch gears at home. It took the first school semester for his school honeymoon period to end.

Conner came to us with such traumatic circumstances and a soul that seemed to have a rejection spirit. After the honeymoon period was over at home, he spent a lot of energy rejecting Randy and me, suspecting that we would eventually reject him. After the honeymoon period, Conner no longer seemed to care what the teachers, administrators, and other students thought of him. Sadly, Conner had developed no real friendships and took advantage of those who reached out to him.

Eventually, as in all relationships, the honeymoon ends and a new version of regular life begins. That can actually be a good thing. But sometimes, new issues surface. It was good for us to remember that, although difficult, relationship-building potential is greater when the honeymoon is over.

Often, our experience was that, after the honeymoon period, a child would begin to reject us simply because we were not their birth parents. The rejection was sometimes something subtle like not wanting to engage in conversation or just being disagreeable. But at times, the rejection was direct, as the child would verbally and sometimes physically express their dislike for us and how they just wanted to go "home." Not all children could or would identify their reason for rejecting us. For the majority of the children though, the rejection was expressed somewhere between the two extremes.

Remember, the child may not have wanted to be moved, so don't take it personally or be surprised when the honeymoon ends. Generally, the child's preference is to be back with their birth parents and they are most likely hoping that they will return home sooner rather than later. I write, "Generally" because at times, a child knows their home of origin is unsafe and they are thankful to be in a new safe and loving home even though they may not express it. I believe that the Lord has placed within each of us a desire to have healthy and close relationships with our parents and even though a child has experienced great trauma from their birth parents, they still love them and desire that close relationship.

I remember meeting at our agency's office to sign the final paperwork with our caseworker Miss Teresa, who had worked with us for several months. I appreciated her helpfulness, companionate nature, and her attention to detail. Mrs. Regina was at the agency's office as well. She was new to me and seemed quiet. She was representing a brother and sister duo. We had previously met Ben and Abby, visiting them at the group home in a different county where they were living at the time. Mrs. Regina had requested a private Christian home for them in a county closer to their birth parents to shorten the driving distance for potential birth parent visits. Ben had already been in two kindergarten classes that year since entering foster care. He acted curious about this new one. Abby had also been in two different middle schools already that school year. She kept her thick dark hair in a top bun and exhibited an "I don't care" attitude.

Most of the arrangements and paperwork had already been completed and Mrs. Regina's car was full with the children's belongings from the group home.

I was not feeling well that day, which was unusual for me. I knew I didn't want to postpone the appointment since it had already been changed by our agency a couple times. Getting all the people and paperwork together at the same time can be cumbersome. While at our agency's office that day, the process took longer than usual. It seems some paperwork had been overlooked and some new paperwork was required. This took place right before lunch on a Friday during the school year. Ben and Abby had said their goodbyes to their classmates and teachers the day before and the group home staff that morning. I had already gone to their respective schools the week before and did as much paperwork and prep as I could in advance of their move.

Randy and I had already discussed that we only had the weekend to acclimate the children to the idea of a new school on Monday. These two children had not only moved from a group home in another county, leaving the adult workers they had come to know there, but had also left a familiar school classroom, teachers, and friends behind. As the two children waited in our agency's office, Abby wept openly. Ben was surprisingly cheerful and appeared excited for the new adventure. Each of these two children were exhibiting different feelings and reactions to the same situation. Finally, the paperwork was complete and we could head toward "home." After stopping by McDonald's for a very late lunch, we visited the elementary school where Ben would begin on Monday. His new teacher was so enthusiastic and led the whole class in welcoming Ben, who acted enthusiastic. By that time, it was almost the end of the school day so we hurried to the middle school to allow Abby to meet her teachers and locate her locker. She was rude to her new teacher Mr. Hill, interrupting him several times about her locker location and locker combination as Mr. Hill was talking with me about what supplies Abby would need on Monday. I was impressed how Mr. Hill took Abby's grumblings in stride.

Once home, Ben engaged with us right away and looked forward to the crock pot dinner I had made earlier that morning, while Abby stayed in her room and continued to cry. After a few minutes, I went into Abby's room and told her we realized she was very sad about being in our home and that she could feel free to cry as much as she needed.

Over the next couple days, Abby wept often and distanced herself from everyone in the home, while Ben awoke daily with a cheerful "good morning." Monday came and it was time to start school. Abby arose early to eat breakfast without further tears before meeting the 6:30 school bus and went to school without visible incident. Ben, who had been so cheerful, had a sudden stomach ache before his 7:00 bus arrived and said he "couldn't go to school."

I usually gave one unannounced "free" day to miss school when a child first came to live with us. Ben, who had started out so cheerful, had many tantrums throughout that Monday while at home with me. I am thankful that I was able to be a stay-at-home mom particularly that day. We made it through the day and Ben's "stomach ache" was miraculously healed by dinner time. Months later, as he still lived with us, Ben and I laughed about that first Monday. He admitted to no real stomach ache and just needing extra time to adjust. And although Ben had much emotional healing ahead of him, it was rare that he didn't continue to come out of his bedroom each morning with a jovial "good morning."

Randy and I read *Exposing the Rejection Spirit* by Mark DeJesus, which was recommended by an artist friend who had read it. She actually lent us her book. The subtitle is *Experience Love – Know Who You Are – Empower Your Relationships*. It sounded like a good tool for us as care givers, as well as useful in our own personal journey. None of us had perfect parents and even great parents sometimes unintentionally reject us. We may even perceive something that wasn't meant to reject us as rejection. I remember my dad encouraging me to make something "useful" with my quilting skills, "...like grandma did... she made bed quilts." But my heart didn't and still doesn't get as much joy from creating bed quilts as it does smaller wall art quilts. My dad didn't intentionally reject me and my desire to create art over bed quilts. I believe he simply didn't understand art quilts.

As I read the book, I not only thought of things from my childhood but it also gave a clearer understanding to things that children in the foster care system had planted into their impressionable hearts. According to the book, adults practice hiding the rejection spirit and pretend it doesn't exist. Randy and I found that most children who came through our home did not recognize a rejection spirit planted in their hearts. Young children in the foster care system who have had great trauma often seek to hide the rejection spirit in their hearts, particularly during the honeymoon period, as they work to not be further rejected. And because of that, we found that the length of the honeymoon period varied depending on how well they hid the wounds deep inside them and the time it took for them to open their hearts to yet another adult.

# CHAPTER FOUR

# ORGANIZATION

I like to think of myself as an organized person. I've sought out tips and ideas from books and friends in an effort to create structure in my home so I can focus on the things that I prefer doing. Paperwork filed away brings me peace as does knowing where things are located when I want to use them. So, I keep things fairly simple in my home. I knew with extra paperwork and meetings required for being a foster parent, I would need to devise a system that would work for me. Although I was organized with my own children, I found being responsible for other children in my home necessitated a bit more planning and consideration.

When our birth children were growing up and most of the time we were foster parents, we lived in a small 980-square-foot home with one bathroom. I loved it. I had to be creative with the space while taking care to only hold on to the most loved and necessary things. This was way before tiny homes and minimalism was popular like it is today. Besides, I don't do well with clutter and tiny knick-knacks that need dusting. They distract me from the things I really want to do like creating art and spending time with people. I find organization is a means to an end that brings a tranquility and calm to our home. I thrive in that. So, I like to keep things simple, flexible, and evolving. Maybe some of my organization tips will help you as well.

I enjoy repurposing items creatively and wanted a different desk. I had always kept our home personal files in a crate with a fabric cover I had made. That worked great until we became foster parents and needed to house personal information of children in our home. It's not like friends and family would rifle through our personal files, but I felt a responsibility to the children in our home to safeguard their personal information. It seemed to give them a sense of security as well. I believe it also helped them know that I valued and protected them in that way. Although our private agency did not require the files to be locked away, I really liked the idea and felt it was worth the extra effort.

I found a used basic desk with a file drawer from an ad and took our truck to pick it up. It was in great condition. Next, I purchased a small drawer lock for under ten dollars that Randy easily installed. The file drawer was now secure and housed all our important papers in one place. We kept the keys to our new locked file drawer securely stashed away in a different room.

I had a few files specifically for keeping organized as a foster parent. I describe how I kept a medical and school folder for each child in more detail in the Drafting a Strong Professional Team chapter. They were also kept in the locked file drawer.

I kept a foster parent file for our certificates of trainings that we had completed toward our license training hours. I liked having a copy of the certificates on-hand in case one of them got misplaced before being recorded in our file with our private agency. That file housed the monthly Attendance Roster Sheet that our agency used to keep track of days the child was in our home or on respite. I've also heard it called a Daily Notes sheet. I usually just filled it out once a month, checking my calendar for any date that we might have had respite that month. The foster parent file also held any other papers I needed to have ready to give to our caseworker when I next saw them. Having all those papers in one place made it easier for me on days when our caseworker would visit. They appreciated my organization as well. Additionally, I kept a current list of contact information for our private agency's supervisors, other foster parents, and the fire marshal.

The first time I tried to locate the number and information for the fire marshal was a challenge. In my county it is a separate office than the actual fire department. So for that reason, I wrote down and kept the information in our home file drawer. Although I knew the fire marshal, Ted, from another setting, I never had a reason to contact him in his professional capacity. Thankfully, someone from our private agency gave me the phone number and I called to make an appointment. It was fairly simple as the county was flexible in arranging a date and time of day that worked with my schedule. Ted called our home en route, which I thought was a clever way to check for a working phone and correct phone number. I had the form from our private agency ready to be filled out and signed so I could turn it in.

When Ted arrived, he checked our fire extinguisher, radon and smoke detectors to be sure they were in working order. He asked when we last replaced the batteries on the radon and smoke detectors. Good question. I didn't know. Beginning that day, I write the date on new batteries with a permanent pen before installing it.

I had carefully drawn out a basic diagram of the inside of our home, including doors and windows, on a sheet of white printer paper for our Evacuation Plan. I labeled the front and back doors as exits with larger windows as the next options. It also had "in case of emergency, dial 911" on the paper along with a diagram of our evacuation meeting location. Our meeting location was at our mailbox at the base of our driveway. Randy's and my smartphone numbers, a neighbor's number, and nearby family numbers were on the Evacuation Plan as well. I placed the Evacuation Plan sheet in a clear sleeve and used a push pin to post it inside one of the kitchen cabinet doors. Ted said that that worked just fine.

In retrospect, I do wish I had asked about all the necessary requirements when I made the initial appointment.

Our small fire extinguisher was not the proper class required for a foster parent home. Ted had to make a second trip out to our home after I purchased the necessary larger fire extinguisher and fresh batteries for the smoke and radon detectors. Lesson learned. Our form was completed, officially signed by the fire marshal, and was ready to submit.

Thankfully, with our birth children, we had never had a fire emergency. Monthly fire drills were something they did at school but we had never done one at home. Looking back, that would have been a good idea. That was about to change when we would have children from the foster care system living in our home. There would also be monthly paperwork required by our state to document each fire drill date, time of day, and the amount of time it took for us all to reach our evacuation location. Of course, it was best to have the fire drills when everyone was at home so we all received the benefit of the practice. Thankfully Randy and I got to decide the timing of the fire drills. Our state required some nighttime fire drills as well. We would usually wait until the children were asleep but before we went to bed to do the night drills. What worked for us was that Randy would push the reset button on the fire alarm and off we would go. I don't know anyone who likes to be woken out of their sleep by a shrill alarm. Getting a frightened and drowsy child out the door and to the mailbox meeting place was often a challenge. Although not fun, it was good to have practiced fire drills in case we did have an emergency.

It took some time to get used to monthly fire drills. In the beginning we often just plain forgot. Then on the last day of the month or before our caseworker would visit, we would squeeze them in. I finally set them as an appointment early in the month on my personal calendar. Even if we didn't get it done that day, it rolled over the next day.

It felt a little weird not having monthly fire drills when we were no longer foster parents although I don't miss them. I often wondered what some of our neighbors thought as they heard our fire alarm, saw us all run out of our home, down the driveway to the mailbox, and then just go back inside. I also wondered what our dog, Susa, thought as she also heard the loud beeping and saw us all running out of the house. I would quickly put her leash on her and we would run to the mailbox together. Susa always seemed happy although a bit confused seeing the big excitement and everyone running. She did receive a dog treat when we were back in the house so she willingly played along.

Interestingly, when a child would come into our home, I'd ask them where they thought a good location might be to meet for our fire drills. Almost every child suggested meeting at the far fence on our property. Actually, that would have trapped us by the fence blocking us from getting to safety. I am glad we had a safe and practiced plan in place. Leaving it up to chance could have had us scattered and potentially in further danger in the event of emergency.

You know the multitude of paperwork that a child comes home with the first week of school? It was handy having all the necessary information in one folder ready to fill out. Actually, depending on the age of the child, I let them fill out their name, our address, phone numbers, and any other information as they could. I found that it helped them become familiar with filling out forms and it helped me out as well. There was one form I never remember seeing when my birth children were in school. Maybe it was there and I just dismissed it. It's a form that has you give information of who is not allowed to come to the school to see or pick up the child. That always felt weird although I understood the reason for it. I made it a habit to personally check with the school office staff to make sure they had the current information, especially when a child first came to live with us. I learned that just because I had sent the correct information back to the school, it may not have been entered into the main system yet.

Officer Thomas, our elementary school's resource officer, called me one day requesting official paperwork about contact information for a nine-year-old Sally who was currently living in our home. He suspected that the contact information on the main county school system was outdated. Officer Thomas was familiar with Sally's birth parents and had doubts about them being able to be contacted in an emergency. I took my folder with the official papers to show that indeed, Sally was in our foster home and her parents were on the do *not* contact list for the school. For whatever reason, the official information had not been updated in the main county system until that day. Having the legal papers available made correcting the error easy.

In our foster parent file, I kept an ongoing list of possible good books to read about raising children and healing trauma. Because I like to learn, I was always on the lookout for book recommendations by trusted friends that might help us help the children in our home. Our private agency would sometimes approve books that I had found, giving us credit hours toward renewing our license. The book choices had to be about parenting children, based on fact, experience, and research. I like to read out loud, so often after a meal or even on a short trip in the car, I could get a few pages read for Randy and me while he drove. I kept a small paper in the book as a bookmark on which I recorded the minutes spent reading. I could then turn that information in along with my and Randy's individually written summary of each chapter. We both found it easier to write our summary of each chapter along the way instead of writing them all at the end of the book. Those minutes added up to valuable hours of learning and credit toward renewing our foster parent license. The beauty was that we could read and absorb the information at our own pace as well as discuss it. Many times, children who were in our home liked to listen to the books that I read out loud also. That was an added bonus. Of course, we read a lot of children's books out loud together too. I've listed some of my favorite books, authors, and educators that you might find helpful as well. Actually, I've read and used many other resources by these authors and organizations and found them to be great!

- *Have a New Kid by Friday: How to Change Your Child's Attitude, Behavior & Character in 5 Days* by Dr. Kevin Leman
- *Bringing Up Boys and The Strong-Willed Child* by Dr. James C. Dobson
- *Boundaries and Boundaries with Kids* by Dr. Henry Cloud and Dr. John Townsend
- *Parenting With Love and Logic* by Foster W. Klein and Jim Fay
- Jim and Charles Fay have numerous resources available online
- *Switch On Your Brain: The Keys to Peak Happiness, Thinking, and Health* by Dr. Caroline Leaf
- *Exposing the Rejection Mindset: Getting to the Root of Our Relationship and Identity Struggles* by Mark DeJesus
- *Healing is a Choice* by Stephen M. Arterburn

Even though it was not necessary to house in the locked file drawer, I kept a file for each child currently in our home of some of their special papers, art, and accomplishments from school that they may want later. I simply liked keeping them with the other folder for the children. Of course, those treasures went with each child if they wanted them as they left our home while the personal and confidential papers were destroyed.

Sometimes children would have cash or gift cards with them when they came to live with us. Depending on their ages, I kept their items safely locked away for them in the file drawer until needed. Each child had a basic manila envelope with their name on it. I liked to write a ledger of sorts on the outside, documenting when and what they spent their money on so there wasn't confusion later.

I had an additional envelope for petty cash which came in handy for paying for extra chores. It also was helpful to have some cash ready for unexpected expenses such as school events. The files and envelopes that lived in our locked file drawer didn't take up much space. They were simply kept together and securely tucked away until I needed them.

Many children came into our home needing to take daily medications that had to be locked up as well. I wanted easier access to them in the kitchen but for them to still be secure. I found a small simple pouch that had a zipper that could be locked and kept it on a high shelf inside a kitchen cabinet. Our local grocery store sold a small thin combination lock which I bought and used to keep the medications secure. I'd reprogram the lock from time to time. I kept the official medication log required for the child folded in that pouch as well as a pen. The medication log was the official paper from our private agency where I had to record the date, time of day, dosage, and my initials daily. It made it simple for me to have the medications, medication log and pen safe all in one place.

Cooking is not my favorite task. And because of that, I'm always looking for ways to eat healthily with minimum effort. I value nourishing meals and snacks because I know it helps our bodies function at their best. I wanted children in our home to have the opportunity to learn the value of eating well and trying new foods. It surprised and saddened me how many children were not used to eating fresh fruits or vegetables.

A few times I tried the method where you cook and freeze meals for the whole month. While I loved the results, the process left me worn out. What has worked for me the best is to cook double for a few nights and freeze the second meal each night for another time. If I am browning ground beef, I prefer to brown a five-pound package and freeze it in small portions. I really like having the meat already prepped for another meal on a busy night. It also means less pan washing, which Randy appreciates since he is the chief pot scrubber.

I like to cook several chicken breasts in my crock pot and freeze them. I make a large pot of spaghetti sauce and divide it into quart-sized bags for later. When Randy grills hot dogs or burgers, he will grill several extra which I freeze and reheat in the microwave another day. I've experimented with freezing various casseroles and discovered the ones we like and others that needed to be prepared fresh. When I'm chopping an onion, I chop the whole thing and store what I don't use right away in a glass jar with a metal canning lid to keep the smell at bay. Some of my experiments work and some do not. Every once in a while, I will make a double batch of a new recipe so I can have another meal already prepared for another day. There have been those times when we decided that a recipe is not a "keeper," knowing we will have it at least one more time since I made two.

My friend Darla is an exceptional cook and has taught me that almost anything can be frozen. I had no idea that chips, nuts, spices, and homemade crispy rice treats would freeze well. Now I also freeze breads, cookies, cookie dough, casseroles, chopped veggies, cooked pasta noodles— and of course my favorite, ice cream.

Randy and I found it helpful to direct the children toward me with food buying or meal suggestions. Thirteen-year-old Kara definitely had her favorite foods when she moved into our home. Sadly, almost all of them were what most would consider junk food and not the best for a growing child. Even though Kara liked the healthy snacks and meals I provided, she missed the junk food she was used to receiving comfort from. I like some junk foods as well but in small quantities. It took Kara a while to realize that Randy and I had organized our roles, with me being over food and meals. Randy made the main decisions about after-school and sports activities since he did the majority of the afternoon pickups after practices. Before that, Kara would complain to Randy about me not buying her preferred junk food in a futile attempt to get her way. It seemed like she was hoping Randy would override me about food. Over time, as Kara settled into accepting my role over the food organization in our home, she complained less and less to Randy. I would often take her to the grocery store with me and let her choose some healthy items that she already liked or wanted to try. I didn't usually take children with me to the grocery store as sometimes it would turn into a battleground. I did often ask children before I went to the store for suggestions of healthy foods that they might like. I am more of an experimenter with food than Randy and would often bring home something new and interesting, yet good for us to try. Some new things were appreciated and liked and some were not.

Most weeks I had a simple meal plan that I posted on an index card under the Evacuation Plan inside the kitchen cabinet. Often, I would ask Kara, as I did the majority of the children in our home, for input into the meals for the week. She seemed to appreciate that, even though every meal wasn't her favorite for the week, the ones that she did like were in the plan.

Phone numbers are easier to organize with smartphones. I organized phone numbers for our caseworkers, their supervisors, etc., in my phone. Often adding notation of our private agency's name or that it was for the children in our home. I found it easier to have them labeled than trying to remember each caseworker's name, especially the ones I had not yet met.

Sadly, I had to add the sheriff's department along with the juvenile justice department's phone numbers at one point. I never considered that would be necessary as a foster parent but it was. Thirteen-year-old Quinn would occasionally run away. He usually didn't go far and I suspected he did it for the attention it brought. Another time, five-year-old Heidi, who had recently entered our home, proudly recited our address that she had memorized to her birth parents on a phone call. The birth parents never came to our home but I felt better being prepared just in case. I also put the sheriff's phone number on a piece of masking tape on our kitchen counter for quicker reference.

It may seem silly or unnecessary but I had a small plastic basket with a handle for each child to store their toiletries. Older children kept their toiletry basket in their bedroom. I had one for Randy and me as well that we kept in our bedroom. So many of the children that came to live in our home weren't good at respecting the boundaries of other people's belongings. Before we began this practice, ten-year-old Elliot did a bit of experimentation with his sixteen-year-old sister Kora's razor. Thankfully, he didn't do any damage but it caused me to rethink toiletries being kept in our one bathroom. Often a younger child's toiletry basket was stored on a high shelf in the hall closet after Elliot chose to test how much toothpaste really was inside the tube.

I felt it was important to help children learn ways to organize their own belongings and their time. Roxy was an agreeable twelve-year-old although she had trouble making decisions that were within her ability to make. Randy and I gave Roxy many opportunities to practice decision making with things like picking out her clothes for the day the night before, choosing to sit on the left or the right in the back seat of the car, and the like. I helped her organize her toys, clothes and books by reminding her that putting like things together would make it easier for her to find them when she wanted them. Roxy really liked having her school things on a particular shelf, which made keeping up with her school library books easier especially on her class's library day.

At first, Roxy didn't like the idea that her bed needed to be made before breakfast. I set the timer one day and told her to make it as slowly as she could. We repeated the timed game again for Roxy to make her bed as fast as she could while still making it neatly. It was literally seconds. I helped Roxy realize that making her bed really wasn't a big deal to accomplish before breakfast. By just spending a few seconds each day, her room would look and feel organized and her brain would be calm instead of chaotic. It was funny that as Roxy practiced organizing and decision making with her belongings, she began to enjoy helping me organize others areas of the home.

I was surprised the first time a child moved into our home that all their belongings were in plastic bags. Each child mostly had little grocery store bags but some also had the large black trash bags. I hated that. It seemed so devaluing to the child. I decided that no child would leave our home with all their possessions in plastic bags. I visited several thrift stores and bought the largest and nicest suitcases available for just a few dollars each. I let my friends know that I was collecting suitcases as well. Our tiny attic housed several sturdy and clean suitcases that were ready when needed. I really believe the children that moved from our home appreciated having luggage to carry their things in to their next home. To me and probably to them as well, it just felt more like they were leaving with more dignity.

I feel like I would be remiss if I didn't mention organizing your finances into a budget that both you and your spouse agree with and work on together. If you are a single parent, it is important to get an accountability partner that will help you. Randy and I spent the first ten years of our marriage not working in tandem with our money. That translated into many disagreements surrounding money decisions. Our pastor at the time gave us a copy of one of Larry Burkett's books on personal finances. Although I read it and found it interesting, I deducted that since we didn't have much money anyway, the principles would not work for us. Of course, I was wrong and when Randy and I did put the biblical principles to work from Larry Burkett's book with our finances, it improved not only our finances but our whole marriage relationship. We worked diligently to get completely out of debt, including our home before our oldest daughter, Melanie, graduated from high school. We went on to be trained as financial coaches to help others since it revolutionized our lives.

Author and personal finance expert Rachel Cruze, who is the daughter of Dave Ramsey, founder of Financial Peace University, writes, "Money is the number one issue married couples fight about, and it's the second leading cause of divorce." Considering the challenges that come with being a foster parent, I am glad that Randy and I were on the same page with our finances before we became foster parents. It also gave us opportunity to model a couple working together and talking out decisions about money without it becoming a big event.

I am a fan of sticky notes, particularly fun or colored ones, but found I would misplace them losing the information they were meant to be saving. So when a friend gave me an artsy covered journal with lots of blank pages in it, I decided to try something new. I began to write down a variety of items in my new journal: notes of projects with my private sewing art students, church notes, my art class sign-up lists, notes from meetings, those I offer art mentoring to, weekly and monthly goals, etc. I sometimes will use a glue stick to add in a special note from a friend. A dried leaf or two can also be found inside my journal. I no longer have to hunt for lists that I stuck here or there or the notes that I took during a meeting. I'm not sure why I didn't do that earlier but I'm glad I started.

I found that the more I was organized in paperwork, food, finances, and things in our home, the more energy and time I had to devote to helping the children feel safe and secure. It may sound trivial, but I believe it spoke loudly to each child that I had our home under control and not in chaos. Demonstrating organization to the children set a standard that they would carry with them to make their own lives going forward simpler. It's funny how things that seem little really add up. For many children who came to us from a home of chaos, a calm and organized home offered them a space to relax and potentially heal.

# CHAPTER FIVE

# BOUNDARIES BUILD BUTTERFLIES

I found it beneficial to think long-term when it came to setting boundaries with the children in our home. Just as a stop light keeps order through a busy intersection, boundaries can help a child avoid unnecessary chaos and help them navigate life successfully. We may not always enjoy setting boundaries yet setting safe boundaries with a child from the beginning deters confusion. It also sets a model of safety and confidence, which allows the child to have space to relax and heal. Not all children will respect and follow your boundaries but it is valuable to set them anyway. The model of setting and honoring boundaries is another tool you can offer a child to add to their backpack of life skills for whatever is next.

I love butterflies and planted butterfly bushes and a variety of flowers that attract them to my yard. As I write this, several Yellow Swallowtails are flitting around the butterfly bushes outside my window. I am especially fascinated by the Monarch butterflies, which are due to migrate through our area in a few weeks. The fact that a lowly caterpillar can transform into a high-flying butterfly intrigues me. I learned that a butterfly's muscles are strengthened as its wings stroke against the boundary of the cocoon. Without that struggle the wings do not develop the strength needed for the butterfly to survive outside of the covering. When allowed to grow stronger through the emerging process, the butterfly will successfully develop the skill to fly free and enjoy its life. I have had the privilege of watching a Monarch emerge from its chrysalis and found it somewhat painful to witness as the creature seemed to need rescuing. Similarly, it was hard to watch children in our home struggle against healthy boundaries. I often reminded myself that the goal was to offer each child an opportunity to grow by experiencing healthy boundaries.

Eight-year-old Rose and her six-year-old sister Violet came for a two-week respite. Rose and Violet had been removed from their birth home a few months prior and were currently living in a kinship placement with their aunt and uncle. A kinship placement is when a relative or very close family friend steps in to care for a child in a safe environment.

We had separate bedrooms for the girls, which was one of their caseworker, Mrs. Carter's, requirements— a boundary, if you will. Mrs. Carter told us that the girls needed space away from each other while they were in respite. One of the boundaries in our home is that you can only go into another person's bedroom with their permission. Knocking or calmly asking was required to enter. If a door was accidently or purposefully locked, we had an emergency door key. That boundary offered a space for each person to have some time to themselves for a break or just to enjoy some alone time. It also provided a safety element for each person's belongings within their room. We found many children were not used to having their belongings safe from others, so most liked that boundary.

Boundaries were foreign for Rose and Violet. They had shared a bedroom and were allowed to go wherever they wanted in their other home until now. I'm not sure if Rose really needed as many breaks from Violet as she took. Maybe she was testing out our system. Either way, Violet particularly got lots of practice having to go back out of Rose's room and ask permission to re-enter. I also coached Rose in realizing that she could choose to say "no" to Violet's persistent requests. This was new territory for both girls and tiring for me. Retraining a child to learn healthy boundaries takes time and practice but I knew the effort was worth it. Over the next couple of days, both Rose and Violet settled into this new boundary routine although it was uncomfortable for each of them for different reasons.

One afternoon after lunch, as each girl went to her respective room for an hour of Solo Time, Rose declared that her hair brush had been stolen. That began a shouting match from the doorway of their bedrooms, with accusing, denying and loud crying. I wasn't sure if Rose had simply misplaced her hair brush or if Violet had snuck in and taken it. I knew for certain that I didn't have it! I let the girls know that I would start the hour of Solo Time when they were calm and quiet and we would revisit the issue afterward. Thankfully, after the hour of Solo Time, Violet confessed to going into Rose's bedroom without permission and taking the hair brush. It was returned along with an encouraged apology and a hug. There were several more skirmishes between the girls before the respite was complete. Each incident brought more peace between them, although I knew it would take more time to solidify the value of boundaries in their minds and hearts. Violet broke Rose's boundaries much less often and Rose found her voice in saying "no."

Another morning after the hair brush incident, the girls had been playing outside nicely. I kept my eyes and ears on them through the open window. For what seemed like just a second, they went out of sight and I heard giggling. I quickly went out to check on them and found them writing words on the door of our truck with a rock from the driveway! Oh boy. Then later in the day, Violet handed me a tiny metal part to something I did not recognize right away. She went on to say that she was sorry for taking it off my sewing machine while I wasn't looking! Oh my. I have no idea when or how she could have taken that part off my sewing machine without us seeing her. I realized that Rose and Violet still had much work to do to learn to respect others' belongings. I also was reminded that things that we valued would sometimes become targets for a child to use against us or to test us. Still, I felt good that we had given both girls the opportunity to try out boundary setting in a safe and loving environment. Two weeks of boundary setting and respecting practice while in our home taught each girl that it was possible.

Thirteen-year-old Tommy was a husky boy about my height with curly brown hair. We first met him when his caseworker, Mr. Oliver, brought him to our home one summer morning. Tommy had been in numerous foster homes and was being placed in our home since we were trained in a therapeutic level of care. A therapeutic level care is for children who need a higher level of care, more structure, supervision, and interventions. In our state at that time, a therapeutic level of training was twice the hours as a regular family level since children classified as therapeutic exhibited more challenging behaviors from their trauma of living with their birth parents.

During that drop-off visit, I read over our home guidelines so everyone could be aware of them and hopefully be on the same page. Our home guidelines also included consequence options if the boundaries or guidelines were not followed. Tommy was mostly quiet with a few "uh huhs" here and there. I sensed Tommy had a strong disrespect for adults but hoped he would grow past that and do well in our home. He had already been removed from the public school in his district, which would require that I drive him to a public alternative school about thirty minutes from our home. It was quickly apparent that Tommy had developed a collection of very foul words and name calling, which he inserted into most sentences he spoke. Randy was clear with Tommy that continuing to use his foul language would bring consequences which seemed to deter the language at first. Tommy had a Guardian Ad Litem, Ms. Clark, whose role was to advocate for him in court proceedings since he was a minor. Tommy complained to Ms. Clark about our language boundary. To our surprise, Ms. Clark called Randy numerous times to defend Tommy's foul language and name calling stating that we were being too strict. In essence, she had chosen to add being Tommy's advocate against us and our home boundaries. Natural consequences of asking Tommy to keep quiet for a short period of time worked at first. Giving extra household chores to give his mind another place to focus worked for a bit as well. Both Randy and I had asked Tommy what worked best to calm himself when he became angry, instead of foul language. He said he really liked being outside and that helped him. So, we would allow him to be outside within the boundary of our acre of property to regain his composure. One evening after dinner, Tommy was particularly agitated about having to be isolated at school as a consequence for fighting with another student. Sadly, Tommy chose to pick fights with other students at school regularly. As Tommy talked to us, saying he had been treated unfairly, he grew angrier. He picked up our fireplace poker and began swinging it at me before throwing it on the floor. He then ran to his room and broke his bedroom door off its hinges. Tommy was out of control and I was frightened.

More than once previously Tommy had gotten a little too close to me and acted as if he would hit me. Our foster care license didn't require me to take self-defense classes but I had taken three on my own and I had let Tommy know that. Still, having someone bigger than me exhibiting unstable behavior in our small living room was scary. Randy suggested Tommy go outside for a bit and cool off and Tommy swung a fist at him. It took Randy off guard, but he spun Tommy around towards the front door, directing him outside. Tommy then apologized and told Randy he was calm and ready to come back inside. But as soon as he neared Randy, Tommy swung again. Tommy had left us no choice. The police were called. We have never had to resort to this before. Flashing lights lit up our property and neighbors began calling to see if we were okay. Tommy took us on an emotional roller coaster that night and we had little sleep. The next day, Tommy spun the story to those at his alternative school that Randy had hit him. That led to a report on Randy being filed with the Department of Social Services. It was all so crazy and so sad. Tommy was immediately placed in a higher level of care to keep him and those around him safe. This was not what we had hoped for Tommy and it was hard not to think we had failed him.

I found peace thinking back over that time and looking for what was true about Randy and me as foster parents. We were good foster parents and had helped Tommy get the additional help he needed at that time. To my surprise, I saw Tommy in a fast-food restaurant a few months after he had left our home. Unfortunately, he was accompanied by two men who were escorting him to a lock-down facility for juveniles. With pain in my heart, I knew that boundaries were still something he needed to learn.

Sabrina was a spunky and fun eight-year-old who won over our hearts right away. Pink was her favorite color and she wore it every day. Once, when she was at our home for one of her many times of respite, she came to the breakfast table wearing a blue shirt. Randy and I gave each other a curious look then we said in unison, "All the pink clothes are dirty". We all laughed and Sabrina asked if she could do her laundry that day. Of course, she could. Sabrina's foster mom had taught her well how to do her laundry. Over all, this little girl was a delight when she was in our home. She loved to go for long walks, play cards, and did chores cheerfully. Randy and I found that as a general rule, most children are on their best behavior when on respite. Sabrina was no exception. Each respite visit is like a honeymoon period of sorts.

Sabrina often didn't sleep well though and would get up in the night but stay quietly in her room. Since I am a fairly light sleeper, I would awake and get Sabrina settled back into her bed. Very early one morning, Sabrina woke up and came out of her room. She was so quiet that I didn't realize it. I startled awake to find her standing over me, cheerfully saying, "Hi, Mrs. Julie!" We had heard of other foster parents installing magnetic door alarms and some families even installed cameras in their homes. I had always felt that those devices were a bit extreme and we chose not to use them. After that surprise awakening, we bought and installed the magnetic door alarms. I came to realize that those simple devices offered a boundary that we all needed. Door alarms come in various sizes and price ranges. We found some inexpensive small ones that did the job. It was basically a magnetic device that could be turned on and off from the outside of the room and would sound an alarm if the door was opened while set to "on." Sabrina needed to be held accountable to the boundary of not coming out of her room at night. And Randy and I needed the peace of mind knowing that she was safely in her room so we could also sleep well. We later installed window alarms as well after we had a different child go out the window.

When children came to our home after that, they usually asked about the door and window alarms. They each tried their best to convince us that we didn't need to set the alarms for them because they were trustworthy. We would explain that the alarms offered peace of mind for everyone. Each child could rest knowing we weren't coming into their room without them being aware while we could know they were where they needed to be. Most children had never considered that the alarm was also for them so that they could rest knowing we weren't coming into their bedroom at night while they slept.

Our dog, Susa, was a brown, long-haired mixed breed who weighed about forty pounds. She loved every child I brought home. I think she considered every one of them her new best friend. She never nipped at a child even when they were a bit rough with her. Kenny was a nine-year-old boy with a strong southern twang to his voice who had lived in a rural country setting most of his life. He was very comfortable around animals and seemed to take a great interest in Susa. He tried, as we all had, to teach Susa to fetch a ball. For whatever reason, Susa never liked the idea of retrieving a ball even though I tried many methods. Kenny was outside with Susa one afternoon as I watched them from the kitchen window. He became frustrated with Susa's noncompliance to his request and pinned her to the ground in his anger. I immediately went outside and Kenny let Susa loose. He denied his deed and, had I not seen it for myself, it would have been easy to believe him. Kenny turned on his sweet voice and was very convincing. I learned that day that not allowing children to be alone with the family pet was a good boundary. Often a family pet is smaller than the child and can become a target for mistreatment. Susa, such a forgiving soul, spent much time after that with Kenny but Randy or I was always with them.

When fourteen-year-old Gwen came to our home, we were told that she needed the boundary of being in a room with an adult unless she was in her own bedroom or the bathroom. It also was suggested that she be required to ask before entering or leaving a room, as was the practice in her home. Gwen had been caught numerous times stealing electronic devices, money, and other items. Honestly, it felt harsh to have to keep that close of an eye on her. And yet, it was for her good, so we agreed. Although Gwen knew the reasons for having an adult keep a constant eye on her, she viewed it as if she was being treated like a younger child. We, as I am sure other adults in Gwen's life before us, reminded her that she could choose to change her behavior and gain wider boundaries. Over time, Gwen would regain a bit of trust and then break trust again by taking another person's belonging. For whatever reason, we found that Gwen seemed to thrive best with tight boundaries.

Being a foster parent can be exhausting and taking time to regroup at the end of the day is a must. Regular respite time is valuable and there's a whole chapter on that. Randy and I found that we needed to build in some time for just the two of us each day. Caring for children that don't always want to be in your home, meetings with caseworkers, regular home visits, forms to keep current, etc., can be draining. We needed time to continue to cultivate our relationship, not only for the sake of our marriage, but so we could be the foster parents the children needed. We wanted time to discuss things without young ears listening. Personal rest time to read or create art and just rejuvenate from the day were mandatory. A mini-respite, if you will. However, we chose to spend that time each day, it was valuable.

Although the time varied from 7:30 p.m. for young children to 8:00 p.m. for older children, having a child in their room for the evening was a boundary that we insisted on in our home. This gave the child the opportunity to finish homework, read a book, or do something quietly before going to sleep. Knowing that you can't really *make* a child go to sleep, we gave them more of an opportunity to wind down before going to sleep by also setting a lights-out time.

The "in your bedroom by 8:00 p.m." wasn't balked at by elementary children but most teens took offense to it. So many children who came into our home had spent lots of time alone but it was not always in a safe environment. Also, many children came from homes where there were very few boundaries and they were used to doing whatever they pleased, whenever they pleased, including staying up as long as they chose.

Millie was sixteen-years-old when she came into our home. She was physically about my size and had a bit of a chip on her shoulder. Millie was making a lot of poor choices in almost every area of her life. One minute, she was laughing and seemed happy and the next minute, she was acting out. It was hard to keep up with her moods. She habitually lied to her teachers about Randy and me and lied to us about her teachers. Millie made it clear that she hated school and did not do her school work.

One of Millie's greatest issues was bedroom time by 8:00 p.m. and she began "discussing" it after dinner the first night after she arrived. Randy and I allowed each child to discuss issues in our home as long as it didn't turn into complaining. If grumbling began, the discussion was ended until the child could re-address the issue rationally. Millie was skillful in her verbal tactics to extend the bedroom time but became angry when it wasn't granted.

We listened to her creative reasons for a couple of nights and set a new boundary of no more discussing this issue. Millie settled in and at least outwardly accepted the bedroom time. I suspected she really appreciated the bedroom time to read but enjoyed the give and take of the discussion. All boundaries don't have to be set in stone. Some nights were later due to special activities or occasions. Over time Millie learned how to better participate in discussions and although she would never have admitted it, I believe she thrived within the boundaries. There is security in knowing the boundaries.

It's been stated that children play freer in a playground with a fence than a playground without a fence. Our goal for children in our home was for them to learn to eventually live freely within the guidelines of this world and that required practice within a loving and safe home setting.

When my birth children were growing up, we lived in a rural area where cars zoomed past on the road. When bike riding or walking, Randy and I set a boundary that everyone had to move completely off of the road and get off their bike when a car approached. We also would allow our children to ride from a particular mailbox to another landmark on their own. Those boundaries increased as the children grew and showed responsibility. They also learned to come home when I blew a whistle. Maybe it was a meal or time to do something else but not coming right away would cause them to lose their bike for a time. These were all good boundaries for their safety and our peace of mind. I would often have neighbors stop and say how much they appreciated how the children got off the road when they passed, as they didn't worry about the children running out into the road.

When you think about it, anything and everything can be a boundary. The key is to pick and choose which things are most important for you and your home. It is your home and you get to choose what issues are valuable and what boundaries can accomplish that. Things like completing chores well before the next activity, homework before any screen time, and eating what's made for dinner or waiting until the next meal are boundaries. Not using kitchen knives or potentially dangerous tools without permission, coming dressed for the day to breakfast, wearing play clothes when outside, asking for permission to get food for a snack are all examples of boundaries that worked within our home. You probably already have many boundaries set in place but have never thought of them as boundaries. They *are* boundaries and have been chosen for the purpose of wellbeing and everyone's good.

Boundaries are something we all have to deal with. We can learn to self-regulate within the boundaries set for us or have them imposed upon us. We get to choose, as there are consequences either way. Our responsibility as foster parents was to offer opportunities for each child to learn to honor our boundaries and to set good boundaries for themselves. The choice was theirs.

Each child was unique and required varying boundaries to keep them safe and accountable. We desired to see each child mature so that some of our boundaries for them could expand. We learned it was important to be consistent with our boundaries and not change them too often, creating confusion for the child. Boundaries are simply a perimeter for everyone's good, encouraging life skills and allowing each person within the home to learn to fly freely like a beautiful butterfly.

# CHAPTER SIX

# TEACHING LIFE SKILLS

We all need certain skills to function well in life. Randy and I found that not every child of various ages who came into our home had been taught even the basics. Honestly, I didn't expect that and was surprised. Because of that, Randy and I found it necessary to never assume what skills a child might have been taught. Teaching life skills, such as personal hygiene, chores, organizing, cooking, cleaning, and other responsibilities, builds a child's confidence in who they are and who they can become. Whether a child's time was to be with us only a couple of days or an undetermined amount of time, we found it important to provide opportunity for them to further grow their life skills level. Life skills can determine a child's success in family relationships, the class room setting, and society in general.

Six-year-old Aria came to our home for a temporary placement while another foster home was being sought out.

She had recently entered the foster care system and was very angry. Although Aria had originally been placed in a home with her younger sister Melody, their combined behaviors were too much to remain in the same foster home. As a general rule, in our state, siblings are kept together if at all possible except in cases like theirs. In her sadness, Aria did not talk much and when she did, she could be hard to understand. So instead of asking a lot of questions, I would say, "Hey, it's time to brush your teeth." Or "Let's brush your hair." As I taught Aria to put her long brown hair into a simple ponytail, she smiled at herself in the mirror. It was one of the first smiles I had seen from her.

Allowing Aria to shampoo her hair and bathe in the bathtub in her bathing suit while I talked her though it made it fun for her. Afterward, she was clean from head to toe and seemed quite pleased with herself. (I would caution you to check with your caseworker as to how they prefer bath time to be handled for each particular child. It can get sticky and although it didn't happen to us, some foster parents have been falsely accused of inappropriate behavior at bath time. Randy and I made sure to have me help the girls and him help the boys with the door partially open to avoid more embarrassment or other issues.)

It was hard to determine if Aria didn't have these skills or was refusing to do them. Either way, as I would brush my teeth alongside her and brush my hair, it gave me a nonthreatening way to see her skill level. It also gave her time with me to see that I was for her and not against her.

I found that gently going over these basic skills as they naturally arose offered grace for Aria to learn without judgment. She was already embarrassed by her situation and now she was being moved to yet another placement. She didn't need her lack of life skills highlighted as well. Plus, we didn't want Aria to be offensive to herself or others due to her lack of personal hygiene.

It became evident that although some of Aria's basic skills were lacking, she wanted to learn. By the time her new placement was identified and set up only ten days later, she had gained valuable skills, was more talkative, and was more confident in the beautiful little girl that she truly was. I learned to not take lightly how valuable teaching life skills is.

Chores and other home responsibilities are also necessary life skills. Research confirms that children who do chores at home do better in the classroom and are more successful as adults. There is so much information about age-appropriate chores available from trusted friends, other books, and the internet. Asking an experienced parenting friend who is also teaching their children life skills can be helpful. Of course, not all children have the same maturity level but I find, in general, most parents underestimate the skills that a child can obtain.

In our home with our four birth children, each of us had daily responsibilities. What worked well for us was dividing up the chores, or "blessings" as I sometimes called them, between the six of us. Yes, that meant Randy and I participated and did chores as well. I felt that having Randy help particularly sent a strong message of leadership and teamwork. Around the mealtime, someone cooked, someone set and cleared the table, someone swept the floor, someone filled the dishwasher, someone emptied the dishwasher and we added feeding the dog and take out the compost to make six things.

As our first-born daughter Melanie got older, she renamed these responsibilities: table manager, floor manager, sink manager, pet manager and dishwasher manager sounded better to her. I simply remained the cook. Regardless of what you call them, everyone having responsibilities around mealtime built the learning of the skill itself along with cooperation and time management.

Twice a week, each person in the household also had a living room and a bathroom job. Again, the responsibilities were divided to not only learn and practice that life skill but to build cooperation. Living room jobs were vacuuming, dusting, straightening the room, taking out the trash, and washing one window of the house. We only had one bathroom at the time so bathroom jobs were tub, tiles, sweep floor, mop floor, sink, and toilet. So that each child could learn and master each cleaning skill, we rotated them weekly on a duty chart that lived in the kitchen. Later we changed that to rotating them monthly for more continuity. The homemade duty chart was nothing fancy. It did have each person's name at the top and the meaning of their name underneath. It was simple but efficient.

As our birth children got older, the skill of trade and barter came into play when a responsibility outside the home overlapped. As each of our birth children went off to college, Randy and I would divide the responsibilities between who was still living at home. I remember a phone call from Melanie just into her first semester of college saying how she couldn't believe some of the other students didn't know how to do basic chores. I took that as a "thank you."

I made a new duty chart when Randy and I entered our foster parenting season. I would research and add each child's name and its meaning to the chart even if the placement was a short one. For most children, it was the first time they had learned what their name meant and they loved seeing it displayed on the duty chart in the kitchen. Depending how many of us were in the house, we again divided up the chores and posted them on the duty chart according to skill level. I kept an index card with a hand-drawn diagram of how I wanted each item set at the table so each child could refer to it when setting the table. Even if a child was only with us for weekend respite, they could put away silverware, set the table, or sweep the floor. They not only saw Randy and I working together but got to participate in the teamwork, which is also a valuable life skill.

Jalen was only two years old when he came one early afternoon for his first two-day respite visit with us. His dark curls didn't hide his fear of being in a new place. His foster mom, Alexis, had come for a two-hour visit with him a week prior to check out our home in hopes of giving Jalen a sense of security. Alexis had been seeking a regular respite home to give Jalen some continuity, which he greatly needed. Alexis was weary and although she needed a break, she wanted to do all she could for Jalen to have a good experience. We had talked of how the weekend would unfold with playing outside, walks, reading books, and helping with chores. Alexis was thrilled we would have Jalen help with chores, reinforcing what she was teaching him in her home as well. As Jalen confidently put away silverware into the correct slots and a few other simple chores, his guard came down with Randy and me. Overall, the weekend was a good experience for all of us. After that, Jalen came for many more respite visits until he was adopted by Alexis. Alexis has taught him many life skills over the years and although we don't see Jalen often, it is great to see that he is growing into quite a responsible and happy young boy.

Thirteen-year-old Roger made it clear right after his DSS caseworker, Ms. Selma, left from bringing him to our home that he was not happy about being with us. He wanted to be back with his dad. And although Roger was shown how to do a few chores over the next few days, he complained loudly, calling me names and stating that we were merely foster parents just to get free child labor. Roger broke the broom, broke the dog dish and told Ms. Selma that we made him wash windows outside in the snow with no shoes and no coat! It's funny now but at the time it was upsetting to be falsely accused. Roger made up many tales to tell his caseworker to get out of doing chores. Chores aside, almost everything was a constant battle and it was clear that Roger was not a good fit for our home. Ms. Selma eventually found Roger another placement.

It's never too early to allow a child to make their bed and tidy up their bedroom. I did find it was easier when the child had less clutter in their room. Remembering *perfect* is not the goal, most children who came through our home seemed to gain confidence in caring for the things in their room.

I enjoy organizing and decluttering so it was natural for me to talk a child through that process, especially Vincent. Vincent came to our home from a group home with an overwhelming amount of clothing, toys, and shoes. Each item seemed to hold a memory or significance bigger than his seven-year-old mind could contain. We learned that originally Vincent had been removed from his birth parents' home at short notice, taking only minimal items with him. Since then, well-meaning adults had gifted him multiple necessities and extras. In actuality, many of the toys were now broken. Vincent had clothes and shoes that fit as well as ones that were way too small and others that were way too big. It seemed that since Vincent had come into the system with almost nothing, he was afraid to part with any of his newly obtained belongings. As he and I talked about how he could bless others with the too small items, he got excited. We went through each type of clothing at a different time. He chose shirts for our first time of cleaning out. He would try on each shirt and tell me if it fit, if he liked it and if he wanted to keep it and why. It became a game of sorts with lots of laughter. I reassured him that even when he cleaned out, he would have enough and that we would get new things as needed. Over time we weeded out the torn and wrong-sized items of cloth-ing. Toys were easier and he kept most all the working ones. I helped him organize them into categories so they were easier for him to access. Vincent expressed to me his thankfulness for helping him clean out his things. This was a new life skill for him although he didn't recognize it that way. It was a lot easier for Vincent to manage the things in his room as we cleared out the excess. Allowing him to take part in this process was giving him a skill long beyond my home. I believe his excessive belongings had become a burden for him.

We finally got around to his shoes in various sizes and conditions. He was able to toss the singles and worn out ones yet when it came to a particular pair of shoes Vincent began to cry. Sob actually. This pair of shoes was obvi-ously way too small as he tried to fit his feet into them. Somehow, he managed to get them on and walk around a bit but they hurt so he quickly took them off. Still he remained adamant that he had to keep them. I never knew the story or memory attached to that particular pair of shoes but Vincent still had them when he left our home many months later.

Yes, I knew it took more time to teach each child to do things I could have easily and quickly done myself.

I kept in mind that we were equipping them for life, not just for their time in our home. I allowed children to learn the basics of washing their clothes, putting them in the dryer, or hanging them out. I knew that allowing a child to fold their own clothes—even if the job wasn't done well—helped them grow in confidence. It was worth the effort.

We also allowed each child to help plan a meal and learn about healthy foods. We have a small fold up step stool that many children have pulled up to the kitchen counter to help stir or add ingredients to a dish. Somehow, just participating in the process of cutting up and arranging fruits and vegetables on a plate encouraged most children to want to try new foods.

Eighteen-year-old Freddy was still in high school when he came to our home. Some states have a special program allowing children who haven't finished high school on time to remain in the foster care system. Freddy was tall and lanky and not very confident about himself. When I mentioned to him that he was going to help with dinner, he let me know that that was "women's work" and "no thanks"! Still Freddy was intrigued and came to help anyway. I'm not sure anyone had offered to let him help cook a meal before then. Even though Freddy talked like he was uninterested, he seemed glad I had asked him. Dirty Rice and Kielbasa is a simple one-pan meal that I had taught my birth children and others who'd lived in my home. I hoped I was setting Freddy up for a successful experience. As I walked him though cutting up the onions and kielbasa, he did well yet verbalized his doubt. He browned the ingredients stirring constantly before adding the spices, rice, and water. A few minutes later he topped the dish with cheese and we sat down to eat. Freddy kept commenting that he wasn't sure why I had trusted him to prepare the meal and how it would be awful and unable to eat.

I had prepared some side foods and set the table. Freddy had a medicine he took before dinner and for some odd reason I put it on my plate ahead of time. That is *never* a good idea for many reasons. I was planning to give it to him right before we ate as I always did. Anyway, we prayed for the meal as usual and Freddy proudly put a large serving on my plate. As I took a bite, I immediately spit it out— the pill had been covered with the food and was now in my mouth. Freddy shouted, "See, I told you I couldn't do it." After I explained what had happened, we all had a good laugh.

The meal was delicious and Freddy was quite proud of himself. He had gained confidence in learning how to cook a main dish and cooked it again on other days. Of course, I had paperwork to fill out about the medicine incident. The recipe for Dirty Rice and Kielbasa is at juliebagamary.com/free-resources.

Freddy was only with us for a few weeks but learned to successfully cook other meals as well. Unbeknownst to us at the time, after Freddy left our home, he enrolled in a local cooking school and I saw his photo in the newspaper as one of their success stories. Yes, taking time to teach basic life skills has value.

Problem solving is a life skill that can be easily overlooked. There is a delicate balance between helping a child maneuver a situation and enabling them to not try at all. One way to look at it is to ask yourself these questions. Could they learn to do this themselves? Do I want to or will I always be around to solve this for them? Could they solve this themselves? There seems to be a belief that since the children in the foster care system have been through so much, we need to rescue them from further hurts and struggles. We didn't and still don't subscribe to that belief. We all have often learned some of our most valuable lessons through having to press onward, figure things out and be creative. There is a sense of elation when we push through and are successful for a good solution. It's that "woohoo I did it" moment that strengthens us and we don't want to withhold that from any child. And yet, like I said, it is a delicate balance because we don't want to further frustrate a child. Seeking wisdom from trusted friends and prayer went a long way in helping us know the difference.

Marie sported a flattering short haircut and exuded much confidence for a thirteen-year-old. Her foster mom, Penny, had been seeking a regular respite provider for Marie and was excited that I loved art.

Marie was very creative in crafts and loved to try new things. She came for respite at our home once a month and often brought her newest craft supplies for us to try.

We got along well most of the time and enjoyed creating together. I had been impressed with how Penny had taught Marie great problem-solving skills. One weekend Marie was working on a project for a book report for school. It was due on Monday and she had barely begun. She had chosen to paint a huge detailed turtle on some poster board but was struggling with it. She wasn't sure how to accomplish what she had envisioned and was feeling her self-imposed time pressure. Frustration turned to tears and Marie began yelling at me. I let her have some time alone away from her project to calm herself. We then talked about her goal for her project, ways she might accomplish it, and the possibility of changing her plan to a simpler one. We talked about why she had waited so long, how that felt, and what she could do differently. Even though it felt like a long weekend, Marie chose to simplify her plan and completed her project before returning home Sunday afternoon. It might have seemed easier at the time to not let Marie struggle and figure things out but I believe that would have set her up to struggle more the next time. Of course, I could have chosen to let her finish her project at home with Penny. Instead, I took the opportunity to allow Marie have another trusted adult help her grow in this life skill. When I told Penny about the weekend, she was thankful I had helped Marie problem solve, which reinforced her learning that at home.

Another important life skill is a simple greeting. Greetings can set the tone of the interaction and help in valuing others. Most have heard the phrase, "you can catch more flies with honey than with vinegar." And who hasn't detected someone trying to "butter you up" because they wanted something from you. Greeting someone pleasantly before asking something from them is just good manners and respectful of the other person. Simply saying, "Good morning" before asking what's for breakfast or what someone can do for you is a good start. That was one of our expectations of children in our home. Walking into a room and saying "hello" or "hi" may seem trivial but it's a great beginning to learning how to build healthy relationships by valuing others.

Randy and I wanted to offer children the life skill of managing money. We did this same practice with our birth children, allowing them to earn and spend money within guidelines. We preferred to have a child blow a small amount of money when they were young rather than a large amount later as an adult.

We kept a list of various jobs that could be done to earn money. These extra tasks were above the normal household duties to contribute to the family unit. And I was sure to check with the foster parents of children who were in our home for respite before offering this to those children.

The level of skills needed for the difference tasks was diverse as was the pay scale. There was something for everyone who wanted to earn a bit of cash. Tasks like washing a window, washing porch chairs, washing the car, vacuuming the car, organizing a requested area, and ironing Randy's work shirts were all options. A child could also suggest a job for pay that we would consider. We would show each child what the job entailed and how to do it so they could have the opportunity of success and reward. We would encourage each child to save for a particular item they desired and work to earn the money for it. Of course, the item had to be something we approved of beforehand.

Joey loved the idea of the job list. Well, maybe more accurately, Joey loved to buy things at the store. To his credit though, this six-year-old was constantly drawing pictures and writing kind notes to Randy and me, his family members, teachers, and friends at school. However, Joey especially enjoyed going to purchase carefully chosen gifts for others. Earning a bit of money allowed him that extra pleasure.

At Joey's previous placement he also was allowed the opportunity to earn money although it became apparent that the standards were different for our home. Randy and I checked each job and expected it to be well done. Pay was given after that. Joey was accustomed to doing a partial job and receiving a lot more money for each job. Randy and I kept our pay scale in line with a minimum wage type amount to help each child learn what they might actually earn when they got a job later on.

Joey went for the highest paying job, washing my car. I was skeptical yet talked him through the process. He excitedly went to put on his swim suit and reappeared ready to start. I helped him gather the bucket, soap, hose, and rags. I showed him that working from the top down worked for me and how to accomplish that. I knew Joey could do a good job if he wanted to but Joey wasn't in the habit of doing a good job. After a few rechecks and some tears, Joey had finally done a great job. He had a great feeling of accomplishment and cash in his hand. I learned to keep cash at the ready in a locked drawer. Joey spent all his earnings at a dollar store, purchasing gifts for others and was quite pleased with himself. Over time, Joey chose to learn to do other extra chores and do them well the first time.

I value thankfulness and find it helps me get perspective when I'm frustrated. Thankfulness is a life skill that can change an attitude quickly. My friend Josie challenged me to join her in starting a thankful journal for myself a few years ago. We were both going through some tough challenges with the children who were placed in our homes at that time. The goal was to write three things each night in our journals that we were thankful for. The goal was not to share our journals but write for our own benefit. Some nights were easier than others as we agreed that we couldn't repeat things. Retraining my brain to look for the positive was a challenge some days. I'm thankful I agreed to Josie's challenge and have kept up that habit even after our foster care season has ended. It has become a valuable life skill for me. Currently, I have a small hand-made journal and pen by my pillow that I write in before going to sleep. I've heard that thinking about positive things before going to sleep helps you rest better. An added bonus. As I have learned to reframe circumstances and events, I find that I am over all better for it.

When we were foster parents, I began a different thankful journal that I pulled out a few mornings a week at breakfast time. Everyone was asked to contribute to the long list of things we were thankful for without too much repetition. This practice was not always greeted with thankfulness but over time it began to retrain how we all thought.

Seven-year-old Emma didn't like the thankful journal idea at first, stating that there was nothing to be thankful for in her life. It was so rewarding to watch as she reluctantly began to participate in adding to the list. Then she began to get excited about the list. Emma began looking for things to add in the journal throughout her day and began asking to write in the thankful journal herself before breakfast. What a delight it was to witness her gradual change in perspective.

Kindness is a life skill. When I was thirteen, I went alone to Sunday school at a nearby church. The "cool" kids went there and I wanted to fit in but for whatever reason, I did not. I don't remember the Sunday school teacher's name so I'll call her Mrs. Grace. I remember how she demonstrated kindness in a way I will never forget. Mrs. Grace was having a sleepover at her house and all the middle school girls were invited. I was excited as I got everything ready to go. My hopes for finally fitting in with the other girls were high plus I loved a sleepover. Mrs. Grace had planned out some fun activities and games. I remember she offered us toasted tuna melts wrapped in foil. Yum! But it seemed every time Mrs. Grace left the room, the girls would say something mean to me. They talked about the pranks they were going to play on whoever went to sleep first. I was scared of being further embarrassed and figured I would be the target of their "innocent" shenanigans. Mrs. Grace would return to the room and say things like, "Now girls, we know how important it is to be kind and show kindness to everyone." She would give biblical examples of people being kind. The next morning as I awoke, dread hit my thoughts as to what the girls had done to me or my belongings while I slept. I am not sure how Mrs. Grace intervened but none of the tricks were on me. Whew. I don't remember any of the games or the biblical examples Mrs. Grace talked about but I still remember her teaching through her words and actions to be kind to others, even those we don't like. Kindness is a valuable life skill that may take a bit of extra time and energy but is worth the effort.

I encourage you to take notice of your daily routine and seek out which life skills are valuable to you. A small thing that may seem normal to you may be just the skill a child in your home could learn that adds value to their lives. Consider how you can incorporate teaching life skills into everything you do.

# CHAPTER SEVEN

# SELF-CARE IS NOT SELFISH

I loved building relationships with each of my biological children individually and collectively. I poured my energy and time into their lives knowing that it would help mold and shape them. As they grew, I was aware that they would be on their own one day and I didn't want to miss a thing while they lived at home. Somewhere along the way, I began to believe the lie that taking time out just for myself was selfish.

Because I love to create, I included my children in many art adventures. One summer, I taught them to dye basket reed and we each wove a small basket. Even though they were in elementary school, their work was impressive. My son Jeremy chose to use his hand-made basket as a project in his fourth-grade class when school resumed in the fall. His teacher remarked about the quality workmanship and suggested that I had created it instead.

I always worked on a hand sewing project that I had brought with me to their soccer or baseball practices and games when I wasn't the official scorekeeper. Waiting at medical appointments, music rehearsals, or riding in the car were great times to set an example of doing something I loved while being present with my family. Taking along handwork may not be self-care for you but it definitely is for me. It slows me down and gives me time to think as well as be present to those around me.

One long car trip to visit family in Florida from our North Carolina home, I underestimated the number of books to read aloud and hand projects for me to work on. Often on a long road trip I would trade my front passenger seat with one of the children for an hour or so at a time to keep things interesting. Well, my son Chris didn't appreciate my extra time without a project in the back seat. He said, "Dad, you need to stop and get mom something to do." And so we stopped at the next exit and I found a small craft kit to work on in the car. At the time, I would not have identified hand work or reading aloud to my family as one form of self-care, but it was. It still is.

I received my first sewing machine as a Christmas gift when I was twelve years old. I quickly read the manual, learned to thread it, and was sewing a stuffed owl kit I had also received by the end of the day. I have been creating fabric art of various kinds ever since and eventually began selling my art. When I create art, I am calm, energized, and focused. After our season of foster parenting, for reasons I didn't understand at the time, I began creating female silhouettes in my art quilts. I realized after creating a few of them that I had subconsciously been working out heart issues through my art. I later called the collection "Honoring Women." I believe creating art of any kind is an excellent tool for self-care.

Where I didn't do so well at self-care was taking time out for myself periodically with just female friends. Oh, I did occasionally but as I mentioned before, I didn't want to miss time with my children. It was hard to see past my children's time living in our home and maintaining a relationship with them. I was well aware that all too soon they would be away at college and with their own future families one day. While I did fun things with other female friends, it was when my children were at school. I don't think I kept a good balance with leaving my children home with Randy for an occasional night out with my friends even though I did at times. I guess I had the fear of missing out with my children. Over time though, I recognized the need for time away with female friends and became more balanced. Honestly, it was uncomfortable at first. I knew the children were fine and in good hands with Randy. I mostly just didn't want my children to grow up thinking I wasn't there for them.

I fought the same struggle with children from the foster care system who came into our home. Maybe even more so. Most of the children who came through our home had not experienced the benefit of strong relationships. A niggling voice inside my head warned me not spend as much time on things I enjoyed. I never knew how long the children from the foster care system would be in our home and I wanted to use that time wisely.

I had heard too many stories of foster parents and adoptive couples who ended up divorcing for various reasons. I did not want to become one of those statistics. I knew Randy and I had to find our methods of self-care, individually and together, during in our foster parenting season.

Usually when we would welcome new children into our home, I would pull back for a few weeks on my personal activities during the day to have time for meetings with caseworkers, doctor appointments, etc. I also limited activities that I did at night although I really didn't go out much at night anyway. I made sure I was home for mealtimes and when the children would go into their rooms for the night.

We were five-year-old Austin's second placement in five months. His placement in a group home before coming into our home just wasn't working out. Dark-haired Austin loved that I began volunteering in his classroom weekly and that I would eat lunch in the cafeteria with him afterward. He didn't actually interact with me as much as his classmates did but he always told me he was thankful I was there and wanted me to come again. Due to some of Austin's challenges, I put a Friday night quilting group that I attended on hold. Austin really needed a lot of consistency and my being home each night to tuck him into bed and read a bedtime story and say a prayer helped him adjust. After about three months, Austin seemed to be settling in. I felt it would be a good time to resume meeting with my quilting friends one Friday night. Austin came home after school on the bus as usual and we took our usual after-school walk to acclimate from school, refresh, and relax. After his one-hour Solo Time, he helped me make dinner. My plan was to wait until shortly before I left at about 6:30 to tell Austin that I was going out for a few hours with my friends. I chose to wait until shortly beforehand since we had learned that Austin worried when he learned of upcoming events too soon before they happened. He would obsess over the details, not trusting the adults to take care of them. My guess is that too often he wasn't able to trust the adults in his birth home, where inconsistency and upheaval were the norm. Often when we had informed Austin about an upcoming happening, he would worry and begin to chatter nonstop trying to work out the details for him and us. That's just too much responsibility for a five-year-old.

I didn't expect Austin's reaction to be as traumatic that evening as it was to my plan to spend a few hours away with my friends. When I told him that I was going to meet with some friends to quilt, he began to cry uncontrollably, asking me when I would be coming back home. When I told him 9 p.m., he asked, "What day?' I was confused. What did he mean, what day? I quickly realized that since his birth parents would often leave him and be gone for several days at a time, leaving him to fend for himself, Austin was afraid I would do the same. It took a while to calm Austin by reminding him that Randy would be home the whole time I would be gone and that what he knew of me was that I was consistent in being where I said I would be. I could have chosen to stay home that night. Instead I used the opportunity to get some needed self-care for myself and model to Austin that after that short time of self-care, I would be back home as planned and on time. I had a good time away with my friends while Austin could get into his bedroom on time. Actually, he peeked out of his bedroom window as I backed into the driveway. He had been watching the clock and waiting for me to get back home. I went in and kissed him goodnight and he settled down to sleep. Being on time is a valuable quality that was reinforced again in my mind that night.

Self-care can look different for each person and it's wise to seek out what works for you. I found asking other foster moms what worked for them helpful too. I realized early on that as a foster mom I had to improve and increase my self-care and sought out ways that worked best for me. Because we raised each of our biological children from birth, they were loved and in a safe home from the beginning. Of course, there were times when they didn't like the way love looked especially when it came to natural consequences or a "no" to something they wanted. Still, they had a base knowledge that we loved them and were looking out for their good. Children who came into our home through the foster care system didn't usually have that loving and safe history in their birth home. We were starting a relationship from a different place with less trust.

I usually was the target for the anger that was within each child as they lived in our home. I learned that children who have experienced great trauma almost always target the foster mom with their unexpressed hurt. Even though it was *normal*, it wasn't fun being a target, but it reinforced my need for more self-care that didn't disrupt the life of the child.

When eleven-year-old Eric came to live with us he was so pleasant at first and almost too agreeable to me particularly. Over the next few days, Eric's pent up anger began spilling out and was targeted toward me in loud, defiance outbursts. He even threatened me with a kitchen knife once. I had chosen to pick him up daily after school for the first few weeks due to his not adjusting well to the other bus students. Generally, we allow children to ride the bus and have that experience. One afternoon, as Eric got into the car after school, his verbal barrage began and I made the decision that that would be the last time I would tolerate being his verbal punching bag. I was taking him to and from school to help him because I cared about him. I determined I would only pick him up going forward for the necessary after school therapy or medical appointments. I needed to care for myself and set a boundary. Thankfully, I was able to set up a carpool with a neighboring parent. We took turns driving both of our children to and from school. Eric was always on good behavior with the other child present whether they rode with me or the other parent. It was a win-win solution that increased my self-care.

Many other foster moms I've talked with share similar stories of being targeted by the children in the foster care system. Those other foster moms would also be exhausted and discouraged by the negativity aimed specifically at them. I made it my habit to observe or ask what was working for them in their self-care. Sadly, most didn't have a plan and felt like they were sinking. Some utilized respite care if and when it was available but most were simply struggling. I found myself brain storming with them for creative solutions for self-care for them and myself.

Meeting at a local park where the children could play and we moms could talk worked sometimes but it was often hard to schedule. When it did work, it was helpful meeting with another foster mom who understood the foster care world so we could encourage each other. I found it equally helpful to meet with other women who were not foster parenting, where the conversation took on different subjects. I needed both and it seemed I was constantly arranging a meetup. Most of the other foster moms I met with expressed their appreciation that I had taken the initiative. Maybe it came easier for me because I was so motivated.

My friend Jane never married and is about ten years older and wiser than I am. We are very different in many ways and I love being around her. She is what I like to call a "fireball." She's energetic, ready for a quick adventure at a moment's notice, so fun to be around, and not afraid to hold me accountable. All characteristics I needed in a friend but was afraid to take the time to cultivate. We became quick friends after a mutual friend introduced us at an event. At the time I seemed to be sinking in the drama with a particular child in our home. I really didn't think I had time for another relationship. As a foster parent, I had already had necessary relationships with caseworkers, pediatricians, child dentists, therapists, supervisors, and other foster parents. I just didn't feel I had the energy for one more relationship but I was so wrong. Jane would invite me over for tea and cookies. She had me at cookies but I wrestled with taking what seemed like frivolous time out from caring for the children in my home. I accepted her invitations and gained so much more than her enticing sweet treats. Jane would look into my situation with fresh, unbiased eyes and help me keep perspective. I came to treasure our time together and her wisdom. She genuinely cared for me, my family, and the children that came through our home. I look back and am so thankful that I made time for that particular relationship. Now I can see it as such great self-care although at the time it seemed so indulgent—especially since Jane always had my favorite home-style cookies, my favorite tea, and a beautiful hand-made mug waiting for my visits.

I was surprised when Jane told me to bring my cooler one evening for my visit. She had made four large containers of soup and took them from her freezer for me to take home. Jane said it was just something she wanted to do for us. Oh, and she had bought a few loaves of specialty bread that would freeze well too. I was shocked, humbled, overwhelmed, and thankful all at the same time.

I used Jane's yummy soup on long days that were full of meetings after school. I would put the soup in the crock pot before picking up children from school for their appointments. What a huge blessing to return home after a full and often stressful afternoon to hot soup and bread ready to eat. Jane continued that habit for the last four years of our foster parenting season! Four years! The self-care part of my time and relationship with Jane was accepting it instead of acting like I didn't need her help. I am so glad I did. Jane and I remain friends still although our relationship has changed. I am in a different season of life now. Jane is dating a nice man currently and is busy otherwise. I love hearing of her new adventures when we talk on the phone. We still make time for tea and cookies but it's less often now. I am so thankful for our friendship and the time we each took to cultivate it.

I also made a commitment to myself during our foster parenting season to begin meeting with a couple different female friends two times a week. It took a while to work out the details of that and it too has evolved over time. I started by making a mental list of emotionally healthy friends seeking to grow in character and relationship as well. Thankfully, I was able to identify several friends who are available on various weeks to choose from. I am past the thought that this is frivolous. I now recognize it as a great way for me to do self-care and hopefully offer care to my friends. We women need each other.

I love to walk so I've made time each week to walk with a friend. My friend Stacie was once a foster mom as well and we prefer to walk on the trails of a local park for an hour about every three to four weeks. I walk with my friend Irene, who is in the medical field, on the trails at a different park. Fridays are Irene's day off so we walk early Friday mornings about once a month. Another friend, Eva, brings her children along while we walk. The children walk, run, or cartwheel up ahead of us giving Eva and me a bit of privacy to chat. I prefer meeting in-person but sometimes schedules and distance prohibit that. Ella, who lives many states away, and I are in the same mentoring group for artists. We met at an event for the group in the spring of 2020. I walk in my neighborhood as we talk on the phone each week at a set time. My resourceful friend Dawn and I go to thrift shops together every few weeks, getting in some valuable girl time as well. Currently I have about ten friends who I get together with over the course of a month when we can work it out. Obviously, we have to remain flexible as some of my friends still have children in their homes and others are traveling with work or other commitments. Still I find that I have to be intentional to set up my goals each week with friend time included. I need it.

Of course, it is valuable self-care time for me to walk alone too. I usually walk up the very steep hill in our mountain neighborhood daily, which gives me a nice time to just think and process life. Sometimes I go early in the morning, sometimes after lunch or dinner. I just know I feel better when I walk in the beauty of the outdoors—it restores and inspires me. It probably sounds like all I do is walk but for me, that is great self-care. It almost seems like the energy I gain helps me to get more accomplished than when I am not walking.

Randy and I also learned to utilize the respite care offered through our private agency. We continually sought the balance of using respite often enough without the children feeling like we were sending them away. I needed respite more than Randy most of the time since I spent most of my time with the children. Thankfully, our private agency caseworkers would often suggest respite for us when they sensed I was needing it. There's a whole chapter on respite.

Eating well is also part of my self-care. Even though I eat fairly healthy foods, I do like sugar and am normally careful how much I eat. Cakes and pies aren't necessarily my thing but I find it hard to turn down ice cream and cookies, especially homemade ones. Oh, and chocolate, especially dark chocolate. You know, quick small bits of sugar. The impact sugar has on me really became evident one afternoon before dinner. Earlier in the day, I had purchased and opened a bag of some small chocolate bite-sized candies. No harm, right? I just ate one here and one there and didn't realize that by dinner time I had made quite a dent in the bag. I didn't grasp its effect on me until Randy came home from work and asked me what was wrong. Nothing, I thought. I told him that it had just been a difficult day, which it had. When Randy noticed the half-empty bag of candy, he made the connection of a steady stream of sugar throughout the day that ended in an emotional collapse for me right before dinner time. I had relied on sugar to comfort me instead of choosing wiser self-care. That was an eye-opening moment.

I began to notice that I was eating more cookies and chocolate when I would allow the hurtful comments and actions of the child in our home to upset me. I needed a new plan. Now that sounds easy right, but it was not. I did know that what I was doing currently wasn't working so I had to change my mindset and actions. I quit buying bags of candy. I know that sounds like deprivation but actually it was self-preservation and I started telling myself that— out loud. For me, eliminating sugar was necessary. Instead, I began cutting up fruit or veggies to have on the counter as a quick and easy snack throughout my day. I realized that I did much better when I had something bite sized ready to eat. I began storing cookies in the freezer so they weren't as accessible. It only takes a minute or two for them to thaw and they are just as delicious. I will admit to eating a few frozen ones just to check it out! I still have to watch my sugar intake and every now and then will give up sugar for a few days to get back to a good balance.

I feel better when I eat well. I also chose to create meals from scratch or mostly from scratch to gain more nutritional value. I made two casseroles at a time and froze one for another night. The crockpot is an easy way to have a wholesome meal ready for a busy afternoon. Depending on the day and the child who was currently in our home, teaching a child to help create the meal was good self-care too. It gave us time together to build relationship and trust. It also helps build them up as they learned a valuable life skill.

One of the reasons that we chose to not take in babies from the foster care system was that I need a lot of sleep. Besides, it seemed everyone wanted the babies and we chose to take the older children who were harder to place. These days I like to get in bed about 10 p.m. to read and write in my thankful journal. I get up about 6:30. When we had children in our home, Randy and I woke up at 5:30 so we could pray together before I had breakfast ready at 6:00. Because of where we lived, ours was one of the first bus stops. The bus came promptly at 6:30 for middle and high school students and 7:00 for elementary school kids. I quickly learned that I had to get to bed a bit earlier so I wouldn't feel exhausted all the time. I chose to exchange the lie of being deprived of staying up late to the truth of taking care of myself so I could care for the children in our home. I actually found that I got more accomplished during the day when I was getting enough sleep. So many of the self-care activities I incorporated have helped me even after our foster care parenting season.

Being selective about what I watched on TV and who I followed on social media made a difference as well. Good self-care for me means setting boundaries on how long I am on social media and what I allow to enter my brain. You may have heard, "garbage in, garbage out." After reading Dr. Caroline Leaf's book, *Switch on Your Brain*, I learned that not only can the brain be adversely affected by negative thoughts, but it affects our physical bodies as well. It fascinated me to read that we can actually rewire our brains by making different choices.

For me as a believer in Christ, self-care is spending time in the Bible and prayer daily. I enjoy using an app on my phone for a daily devotion. It keeps me focused on what is true.

A while ago, I began a quest to seek out lies that I believed about myself. It has been so freeing to identify those lies and replace them with truth from the Bible. It has renewed my mind.

I found that even subtle lies like, "I'm *just* a foster mom," "My opinion doesn't matter," or "I'm not good enough" affected many parts of my life. They had to go! I discovered truths and actually have written the truths on an index card to read aloud to myself daily. I keep the index card beside my daily vitamins, which helps me remember. I call them my daily affirmations. One of my current affirmations that I have kept since our foster parenting season is, "I am a fun Nana, a loving mother, and a faithful wife." "I am a loving mother" was particularly helpful when a child would lash out at me verbally. It helped me remember who I really am.

We began including the children in our home in this practice of writing affirmations, helping them identify lies they believed about themselves and replacing them with truth. Statements like, "I am valuable," "I am able to learn," and "I am loved" brought remarkable differences to their brains and actions. Each child was encouraged to create and write their own affirmations. Often, they would read them aloud with mixed emotions about the validity of them but that was OK. Retraining the brain takes time and has to start somewhere.

I found my daily affirmations to be quite powerful for my self-care especially when a child would hurl their words of hatred toward me. As children in our home also began the simple practice of reading their affirmations daily, it helped build the child's self-esteem as they rehearsed truths about themselves. Five-year-old Austin, who I talked about earlier, particularly enjoyed saying his affirmations. He also wrote them in his journal and kept adding to them.

Over time I learned to quickly reframe a child's hurtful words by reminding myself it wasn't necessarily toward me. At times, depending on the particular child, I could talk that through with them to help them realize their anger wasn't toward me but their birth mom. Of course, there were times when they simply didn't get their way, they really were mad at me personally. Even then, I learned to recognize the anger as what it was and not take it personally. Reframing hurtful thoughts was good self-care for me.

I developed the habit of writing a weekly email update for the current child in our home and sent it to the caseworker, supervisor, and therapist. I sent it to everyone at once so everyone could get the same information and I didn't have to tell updates individually when I saw them in person. That was self-care for me. Our caseworkers appreciated it too. Every once in a while, I'd read back over some of the updates I had written. It helped me see progress that a child had made while in my home and under my care. That was encouraging. It also helped me see regressions of some of the children so we could be aware and address the issues.

My friend Lyla is a spunky mom with four teenagers. Two are biological and two are adopted from China. Lyla is witty and great with words. She often writes a blog describing a recent situation that has occurred in their family. Humor is one of Lyla's ways of self-care and processing the challenges of raising a blended family. I love how she reframes her recent events using humor to lighten things up. Others, including myself, often benefit from Lyla's method of processing events in her home.

I'm finding that writing this book has become self-care for me after our foster care season. Some of our placements and respites were close together in time—with many being back to back. That made it a challenge to process things for myself. My heart went out to every child who came through our home and their lives of trauma affected me as well. Living with the after effects of each child's experience broke my heart. Learning the stories of what they had lived through was sometimes more than my brain could process. Of course, we knew we would usually only learn parts of their stories. So many children hide the whole story as it's often too scary to admit, let alone talk about. Caseworkers don't always tell you the whole story either. Maybe they don't know it all, maybe they only have second-hand information, and maybe much of it is "confidential." Perhaps a child discontinued certain behavior so the caseworker may see it as not relevant any longer. Sadly, sometimes a past behavior will reappear with a change in placement. I also think, at times, that a caseworker not telling the whole story about a child gave the child a fresh start. Whatever the reason, there was a lot of trauma that came into my home and hearts that needed mending. Thinking this through and writing it out is further healing for my own heart and mind.

There were periods of time during my foster parenting season that I sought out Christian counseling for myself. It was natural that living with children who had experienced such trauma brought up issues from my own life as well. Sadly, I usually waited until I felt desperate in processing it all to make an appointment with a counselor. Somehow, I felt that that I should be able to process it on my own. That was another lie I had to dispel. I began asking around to trusted friends for suggestions. I knew I wanted a counselor who held the same spiritual values as I did and one who would be gracefully honest. I also knew I didn't want to be in therapy forever. I simply wanted to heal and gain more tools in self-care to be a better equipped person and foster mom.

I met and interviewed a couple counselors before I met Bonnie. Bonnie was experienced in working with foster and adoptive families, soft spoken and had a close relationship with the Lord. Just describing why I was there for an appointment on the forms before my visit was emotional.

And then there was the payment.... gulp. Was I really going to spend that much money for each session? I decided my peace was worth it. I began meeting with Bonnie twice a month at first. I cried through most of the first sessions as I spilled out the hurts within my heart. I confidentially shared the trauma I was dealing with from the children in my home.

There is a misconception, a lie really, that if you just love the child *enough*—whatever that is—they will heal. Love absolutely can be healing and I knew we had plenty of that to share. But trauma affects the brain deeply so additional tools are needed. There has to be a desire to heal and, sadly, most children who came through our home did not have that desire. The need to heal would point to a reason for healing. Most children seemed to feel they would be disloyal to their parents if they admitted any wrongdoing. It was a vicious cycle that was so hard to watch.

My sessions with Bonnie were quite healing for me as she directed me to truth about myself and taught me to look at situations with a fresh perspective.

People said to us many times that we must be super saints to take in foster care children and how the children will one day thank us. Sometimes I just wanted to scream! We were *not* super saints and most of the children did not thank us. They were hurting so much themselves. Usually they didn't want to be anywhere near foster care or living in a foster care home no matter how much love we offered. Our home often was a reminder of their parents' lack of care for them. Bonnie said none of that super saint stuff. Bonnie listened well, empathized, and gave me space to process without judgment. Bonnie gave me the freedom to dig deep and explore where the hurts of the children in my home were bringing up things in my own heart that needed healing. Each session seemed to end too soon yet I was thankful for the tools I gained. Over time Bonnie and I created a friendship that went beyond the counseling sessions. We still meet every now and then to walk and talk.

Naturally, it's important that Randy and I take time out for ourselves on a regular basis. I'm not about a fancy dinner out. I actually prefer a picnic and a hike or takeout pizza eaten by the lake. There were days when going to the grocery store was our time together. It was good just to be with each other. I also now enjoy the time we have in the car together as we travel to see our grandkids. Randy still loves to drive and I still love to read aloud and sew en route. I've told Randy for years that if we simply hold hands while we are out and about doing seemingly normal things, it counts as a date. He doesn't quite understand that but still holds my hand. One day I want to be one of those really old couples I see walking side by side, holding hands and still in love with each other.

I can't imagine how I would have coped without my activities of self-care during our foster care season. Foster parent or not, the self-care skills I've learned and continue to implement have been so valuable. The investments I've made in self-care have been worth it after all. Some of the things I've tried have worked for a time and some have not. I find that when I purposefully changed my mindset on my need for self-care, I became more determined to make sure it was a part of my day every day. That means that I also have had to set boundaries on things that aren't the best for me so I make time for the ones that are. It's called *choosing the best over good*. Self-care isn't selfish because it helps me be a better me so I can be of service to others.

# CHAPTER EIGHT

# EVERYONE NEEDS A BREAK – RESPITE CARE

For whatever reason, I had never encountered the word "respite" prior to hearing it in reference to a foster care system service. Once we became foster parents, I learned that respite is a time or interval of rest or relief. As a young mom, I knew I needed a break. I would have loved to have a whole day off to myself. Having a date with my husband was a rarity. Having a night off and leisurely waking up without little ones who needed my care would have occasionally been wonderful. As much as I enjoyed parenting our four active children, living states away from our family made a break or a respite seemingly impossible or so I thought. At times, we would ask friends from church to care for one or two of our children and they would. Yet, understandably, it is rare for a family to take on four energetic siblings or for the siblings to be all away at the same time. And then there was the consideration of who to even ask, not wanting to be a burden on anyone. The children were of course our responsibility so I had such mixed feelings of guilt and knowing I needed a break once in a while.

Randy and I were very aware of how fast our four children were growing up and we wanted to take every opportunity to build relationship with them as much as possible while we still had them in our home. We knew we didn't want just anyone caring for our children so we didn't often ask for help. Paying for a sitter was expensive for four children so we rarely chose that option. We mostly took turns giving each other a break but seldom took a break together.

Admittedly, Randy and I didn't do well taking breaks for ourselves when our children were young. I look back now and wonder if all our "reasons" for not seeking a break were really just "excuses." Thankfully, we realized over time that having a respite was good for everyone. A date night for just the two of us was important to building our marriage relationship as well. One day our children would be grown, move away, and have homes and families of their own. We wanted our marriage to still be a good one and that takes time.

I can remember being at a special weekend event at church with all four of our birth children while Randy was working. I mentioned to one of the speakers that I didn't know very well that I was exhausted and needed a break. Unbeknownst to me, that person mentioned it to a small group leader in our church who took up a collection.

They gave us enough money to pay for two trusted teen girls from our church to watch our children under the supervision of their parents in their home. There was also enough money collected for Randy and me to pay to go to a local bed and breakfast and for some meals out for the weekend as well. I was overwhelmed and a bit embarrassed by their generosity and desire to give us a much-needed break. I also realized that others saw we needed a break and were willing to help us when we asked. Honestly, it felt weird getting away without the children even though we only went to the next town. Our van broke down on the way but once we got it home and got our other car, we were on our way to a relaxing and refreshing weekend. A respite.

All our birth children were out of our home when we received our foster parent license. Learning that the need for respite care was great within the foster parent community we were excited when our caseworker, Wade, suggested we give another foster parent couple a weekend of respite. Because of my past experience with not taking regular respite, I had a special place in my heart to offer it to other foster parents.

Wade set it up for us to offer a weekend respite to a young foster couple Miguel and Ana right away. We met them in a McDonald's parking lot on a Friday afternoon about midway between our two homes and got briefly acquainted. We had only met briefly over the phone so it seemed a bit odd that they were handing over the two young Hispanic boys, Juan, age three, and Carlos, age five, that they were caring for in their home. In reality, they trusted our foster care agency who trusted us. It was obvious to me that they were exhausted and in need of a break. After having four children, three of them boys, I thought two little boys should be fairly easy.

Juan and Carlos didn't talk much at first as they did not know us and they did not speak much English. I wondered what they thought, meeting in a parking lot with their little weekend bags to go stay with strangers who did not speak Spanish. Oh, I knew a few phrases but I was sure that wouldn't go very far. Shortly after returning to our home with these two precious boys, it was evident that they had a lot of anger inside them. There were tantrums, crying, and hitting. The weekend was harder than expected and indeed my few Spanish phrases either did not apply or fell flat. Playing outside a lot and going on several walks seemed to help. When we met Miguel and Ana again at the same McDonald's parking lot on Sunday afternoon, they looked renewed, rested, and ready to begin again. They were very appreciative while Juan and Carlos were glad to be heading back home with foster parents, they knew much better than us. We knew that our part in offering respite, even though a challenging weekend for us, helped Miguel and Ana's ability to care for Juan and Carlos.

Within our private agency, we foster parents could request respite and our caseworker would work to arrange it, based on which foster parents were available and willing to offer respite when we requested it. Our private agency paid the respite foster parents a set fee for each day of respite. I learned that sometimes Medicaid pays the respite foster parents instead. I liked the fact that foster parents were able to receive the respite care without charge to them.

Realizing the importance and necessity of respite, we offered it almost every weekend for a while and sometimes during the week. It not only gave other foster parents a needed break but helped us see more of some of the challenges of having children from the foster care system while they were in our home. Over time, we became the respite providers requested by the same foster parents whose children seemed to fit well in our home. This made us a valuable part of the foster family's team.

When Randy and I were on the receiving end of respite for the children in our home, we learned that not all respite providers were a good fit for our family or the child we had in our home. We experienced a few respite providers that did not offer the level of consistency that we desired and some that made the child's time away like what I call "Candyland." Candyland respite reminded me of separated parents where one offers safety in guidelines and the other wants to only be the entertaining and fun parent. We found that a Candyland respite left the children resenting the structure in our home. Those type of respites took several days to undo; sometimes it seemed easier to not have respite than to have to work so much harder afterward to get the children back to normal life in our home.

We had one respite provider for a child in our home who we later called the Cat Lady. Our caseworker at the time, Mrs. Eva, set up a weekend respite for us for dark-haired, handsome, twelve-year-old Davon, currently living in our home. Davon didn't like change and made it clear that he was not in favor of going to respite with someone he had never met. Actually, Davon didn't want to go to respite at all. Normally, I prefer meeting the respite provider with the child in a public place during the daytime. That allows the child to meet the respite provider and adjust to their home, usually have dinner with them a few hours before they are tired and ready for bed. In this situation, Davon had an event at his middle school that ended at about 8:00 p.m. The adults agreed that it would be fine to give Davon the opportunity to participate in his event before respite. After the event, in the dark, I drove toward the respite provider's home in a location I was not familiar with. Most of the way there, Davon kept saying he didn't want to go to respite and please just let him go home with me. I knew I needed a break and trusted that the respite provider would be a good thing once we arrived. The Cat Lady lived in a multiple-building apartment complex that wasn't labeled extremely well especially in the dark. I got a bit turned around but finally found the correct apartment. When Davon and I walked into the Cat Lady's apartment, a strong smell of cat urine hit our noses. As the Cat Lady and I began to talk, Davon began to cry and asked me to please not leave him there. In fact, Davon repeated over and over that he didn't want to stay and "please, please just let me go home with you." Knowing that each foster parent and their home has been checked out for safety, I was confident he would be safe even though it was awkward. Davon stormed off to his weekend bedroom and slammed the door. I left. Once in my car, I tearfully prayed on the way home for Davon and the Cat Lady to have a good, safe, and restful weekend. Thankfully the weekend went well although Davon requested to not return there for respite again. Randy and I had a restful weekend while Davon was in a safe place. I did let our caseworker know about the strong cat smell and unkemptness of the apartment the following Monday. I requested a different respite provider for the next time.

It wasn't uncommon for us to offer respite for another foster family over a holiday giving the other foster parents an extended break and time to be with their own families. Our four birth children welcomed whichever children we had living with us so we would just have a bigger family celebration at one of our homes.

Respite needs can be great so we doubled up one year over Thanksgiving break. Fourteen-year-old Eric and eight-year-old Mason were in separate foster homes but knew each other already and got along very well. We had planned to have a quiet Thanksgiving at home since all our birth children and their families had plans elsewhere with their in-laws. At the last minute, our birth son, Chris called and invited all of us to come up to his house on Wednesday and travel back to our house late Thursday. Their plans had changed. I tried to contact our caseworker but was unable to connect, so I left a message. This was before cell phones. I figured it probably would not be big deal and would be approved anyway since Chris and his family lived only an hour away. Randy, Eric, Mason, and I had a wonderful time with our son and his family, then spent the rest of the weekend respite at our own home. What I did not think about was that to get to Chris' home, we had to cross over the state line. Since we had never taken children in the foster care system across state lines, we did not know that we were required to have a signed transport form and a consent to treat in case of emergency form with the location of the destination printed on it. Oh dear. Our caseworker gave us paperwork to fill out after the respite stating what we had done and what we needed to do in the future. More paperwork. Lesson learned. Always get written permission in advance.

We had a long stretch of time when we didn't have children from foster care in our home so we offered a respite weekend for a tall and lanky fourteen-year-old girl, Shawntee, one weekend a month. Shawntee's foster mom's caseworker was seeking a regular respite provider for her and had not found one yet. Shawntee loved to create art and when we met in a local grocery store parking lot, her foster mom, Linda described me as "the craft lady I told you about." Shawntee got into my car and we headed to my home. On the ride home after picking up a child for respite, I would usually ask them about their hobbies, interests, favorite school class, etc. I would tell them a bit about Randy so they were not surprised to see him when we arrived back at my home. I also mentioned our dog, Susa, and how she loved every child I brought home.

Shawntee enjoyed being with us for a quiet weekend, playing cards, taking several long walks, and doing a bit of crafting. On Sunday afternoon when we met for the exchange, Linda asked how it went. I told her it went well. She timidly asked if we would be willing to have Shawntee again and I said "sure." Linda was very excited and said "great, I'll let my caseworker know so we can set it up again for next month!" Over time, Linda shared with me that as a single foster mom, having respite once a month allowed her to continue giving great care to Shawntee.

In her foster home, Shawntee exhibited some challenging behaviors that we rarely saw in respite. I know this because Shawntee would talk about them. Maybe since as respite providers, we were not her foster parents, she didn't feel the need to rebel against the rules. I don't know. I do know that we would take every opportunity to verbally affirm and validate the foster parents in front of each child who came to our home for respite.

Shawntee's foster mom Linda told me how appreciative she was, how our respite provision was a great fit and that we followed the guidelines that she requested while Shawntee was in our home. Not every weekend respite with Shawntee was as pleasant as that first one. Overall, through many walks and craft projects, we really did build somewhat of a bond. I was honored to be invited to the intimate ceremony at Linda's home when her adoption of Shawntee was finalized. I like to think that Randy and I had a part in the success of Shawntee's foster care experience that led to her adoption. Shawntee is a young adult now living out on her own. Once in a while, I will see her in the grocery store. I also make a point to occasionally go by her place of work just to say "hi" when I am in that area. It's fun to see how she has grown into a contributing member of society from the sad trauma that put her in our path in the first place.

During that same period of time we offered monthly respite to seemingly shy two-year-old blonde David for several months one weekend at a time. David took a long time to really trust us due to his circumstances before entering foster care. The first weekend David was with us for respite, I took him on a walk on a neighboring gravel driveway through the woods to a vacant neighbors' summer home. We had permission to walk there from the owners. It was safe, away from the main road and the owners only came up to their summer home a few weeks out of the year. Of course, Susa always went with us. David liked Susa and they seemed to be friends right away. David was fairly quiet and didn't want to walk next to me. Remember David was two! That was fine since we were in a secure area and I could give him some space. Along the way as we were returning home, David just stopped and couldn't seem to move forward. He wasn't tired. He wasn't crying. He most likely had been triggered by something unknown to me and was frozen still. After several minutes of me talking with him and gently taking his hand, David relaxed and walked back home with me. I never knew what triggered David. He may not have known either. Over time, our consistency with David allowed him to finally trust us more. David loved playing with Randy and "helping" him with things in the yard. We built a relationship with David one weekend at a time as his foster parents, Simon and Kacey, got a needed break. A few months later, David was adopted by Simon and Kacey. I had the privilege to create a commissioned adoption fabric art wall hanging for them that hangs in their living room as a keepsake. For their commissioned art piece, Kacey chose a bouquet of fabric flowers, with each flower representing the members of their new immediate family. How appropriate.

Kacey and I have continued our friendship although mostly through social media. It delights me to see photos of David and how he continues to heal and grow. Every once in a while, I will see David in person and it is a pleasure to see him doing so well. Respite matters. As important as it is to be a great foster parent, you can also be a great foster parent who offers respite that aids other foster parents to be successful as well.

## Respite Delivery and Pick Up

After our caseworker would make preparations for each respite, they would give each set of foster parents contact information so we could work out further arrangements. Sometimes when needed, an available social worker would help with delivery and pick up for the respite. I found that making detailed arrangements before the delivery time can take a lot of the guesswork and anxiety out of the exchange for both the adults and the children. I preferred to chat with the other foster parent either by phone, text, or email to find out about them and their home before the respite time as well. Even when meeting in a public parking lot, playground, or a park, it was helpful to specify where to meet in that parking lot. More than once I have been waiting on the opposite side of a parking lot from the foster parent I'm looking for. It also helped to give a description of our car.

Once, after setting up all the details of respite with a foster parent, Mrs. Johnson, I arrived with a red-haired teen boy, Brian, and his enthusiastic younger sister, Hannah, at the appointed spot a bit early as was my habit. I knew from our phone conversation that the other foster family had a specific red vehicle. So there we were, both children and me waiting in the parking lot of an agreed upon restaurant. I was thankful when that red vehicle arrived shortly afterward. She parked and promptly went *inside* the restaurant which surprised me. We had agreed to meet in the parking lot. So, Brian, Hannah, and I got out of my car, went inside and found her seated at a table. I asked if she was Mrs. Johnson and she said "yes." I introduced myself, Brian, and Hannah while she sat looking at us quite perplexed. It quickly became apparent that she was *not* the Mrs. Johnson respite provider we were there to meet. I remember the other patrons of the restaurant looking on as the situation became more awkward. I apologized. Very embarrassed, I walked with Brian and Hannah back to my car as we began to laugh to tears about the absurdity of it. I mean, what are the chances of a lady with the same name and same vehicle coming to the same restaurant at the same time! We giggled and imagined what Mrs. Johnson sitting in the restaurant must have thought of a woman following her into the restaurant and offering for her to take Brian and Hannah for the weekend. I'm laughing again as I write this. We waited for a few more minutes when the correct Mrs. Johnson arrived right on time. Of course, we told her our story of the other lady and her red vehicle, still in the parking lot. Brian and Hannah went with this Mrs. Johnson and had a good weekend. That particular respite weekend was a good fit for us and the children and one we requested again.

Remember earlier when I mentioned how this whole book began by asking my mentor Matt how to publish my list of respite guidelines? I had created a list of some respite guidelines that worked well for us and other foster parents we knew. Many people have requested these guidelines and I thought you might like to have them too. Here's this list.

- Remember, the goal of respite is to give the foster parents a rest, not to entertain the child.

- Ask the other foster parents their preferences for respite care and generally what works best with these children.
- Follow the foster parents' suggestions as closely as possible.
- Follow the foster parents' home schedule as closely as possible for mealtimes, solo times, rest/nap times, and bedtimes.
- Be on time for delivery and pick up of the child at the specific location agreed upon by you and the other foster parents. Consider meeting at a park, public place, or agency office.
- Allow a few minutes for the exchange for a smooth transition.
- Expect the child to address you as Mr., Ms., or Mrs. _____ and not your first name alone to establish authority.
- Communicate your house rules/guidelines clearly to the child in the presence of the foster parents to establish adult unity and clarity.
- Be prepared to accommodate for valid food or food dye allergies.
- Avoid sugar or special food treats so the other foster parents and child can bond in that way at home.
- Ask for and obtain in writing instructions for any medicines. Be sure medicines are in original medicine bottles with original dispensing instructions. Fill out the required paperwork when giving medicines.

- Simple activities like taking walks, working puzzles, yard work, and your normal chores exhibit real-life expectations. Continue your normal life during respite and expect the child to help with home responsibilities like sweeping, cooking, and age-appropriate clean up. Check with the other foster parents to see what the child currently does at home.
- Expect the child to keep their area tidy and continue their daily hygiene as they would at home.
- Pleasing the child is not the goal. Be strong in the guidelines you agreed upon with the other foster parents.
- Don't ask questions you already know the answer to, which can give the child an opportunity to lie.
- Don't be the "Candy Land" type respite, remembering that bonding with the other foster parents is the goal.
- Respite is an excellent time to pass along a skill or hobby you have. Think gardening, woodworking, your favorite hobby, creating art, or other valuable life skills.
- Respite is not necessarily a time for the child to bond with the respite providers. Instead, respite providers should build on and enforce what the other foster parents are doing within their home.

## After Foster Care Respite

After twelve years of foster parenting, Randy and I chose not to renew our license as foster parents. We began getting several requests to offer respite for children who had been adopted. After a child has been adopted, they are no longer in the foster care system and are no longer offered respite within the foster care system. The need for respite is still great for adopted children as being adopted doesn't automatically remove hurts and trauma. Because of our many years parenting our own children and many years of training and being therapeutic foster parents, we realized that we had a great skill set to offer children who had been adopted. We personally prefer to only offer respite to children of families we know and who have similar family values to ours. We don't have paperwork to fill out for the foster care system because adopted children are no longer in that system. We choose to only offer a few hours' daytime respite now and not overnight respite although there is still a need for that. Each family has to decide what works best for them.

One of our first experiences of offering respite to an adopted child was with a beautiful thirteen-year-old Liberian girl, Katy, who is as tall as I am. Although she is very athletic, a great gymnast and good at acting, Katy has some special needs. Her parents are great and love her so much. I have talked extensively with her mom, Lena, concerning how to have respite here at our home that is helpful to them and safe for Katy. I charge a set amount per hour, which keeps everything professional. Many families like Katy's apply for and receive funds from their state or a grant specifically for respite care after adoption that can be used to cover respite fees. Due to the intensity of Katy's needs, we usually offer respite once a week, usually on the same day of the week for about four hours. Having that consistency gives Lena a regular break knowing that Katy is safe and in our trusted care. Right before Katy comes for respite, I remove everything from the guest bathroom except the toilet paper, soap and hand towel. One of us is always in the same room with Katy while she is with us. We usually will take a long walk while she is here giving us both some exercise. Since Katy is homeschooled, she often brings her school work and does it at our kitchen table. Some days I'm not sure she is actually doing her school work but her mom and I have agreed that making sure she does her school work is not part of my role for the respite. I stay near Katy and either read, prepare food, or do some hand sewing. When she doesn't have school work or reading, we might do a bit of yardwork or just enjoy being outside. Regular things. Nothing special. While Katy is here, I rarely contact Lena for anything, giving her a true break without feeling like she has to check her phone for updates. That allows Lena to relax and use her time of respite however she wants without interruption. It's just four hours. Actually, it was our habit to not contact the foster parent either when we were offering respite through the foster care agency for the same reason. If there was an emergency, we would call our caseworker instead.

A few months ago, Lena requested that half of the four-hour respite time be for sewing lessons. I was skeptical at first since, although pleasant, Katy rarely talked to me while she was here and seemed to resent the fact that Lena had respite. But I agreed to try sewing lessons with Katy. We began where I normally begin with my young sewing students. I taught Katy to create an eight-inch by eight-inch hand embroidered piece of art incorporating her own actual hand shape. Katy learned to thread a needle, which was not easy for her. She also learned to tie a small knot at the end of the thread. Also, not easy for her. Although at first Katy struggled with threading the needle and tying a knot, tracing her own hand onto fabric made the piece personal and Katy seemed to like that. Over the next few weeks, Katy learned and mastered quite a variety of hand embroidery stitches and the hand sewing skills I taught her. I was impressed. Katy also smiled and talked more when she was here whether we were sewing together or not. She made it a point to thank me for teaching her sewing skills and to let me know she wanted to learn more. Lena noticed the difference as well since Katy began to look forward to her respite with sewing time here. Katy asked if she could learn to sew on a sewing machine next. Yikes. A sewing machine has a motor and the needle moves much faster than the hand-held one that Katy poked herself with many times. I told Lena we could try it since Katy's grandma had recently bought her a sewing machine. We started from the beginning again, learning how to thread the needle for the machine. Together, Katy and I sewed some very basic things. I love how Katy's grandma continued to encourage this new avenue of life skills, sending Katy fabric and a book of doll clothing patterns through the mail. I'd never sewn doll clothes, so we learned that together. Katy still continues to excel in sewing and I have been so impressed with her change in demeanor while she is here. I recently told her mom Lena, "Katy is like a different kid when she is sewing." For now, sewing seems to be a positive growth place for Katy that is helping her brain to relax and heal. Sewing is also offering Katy a life skill and an area of confidence that she can do at home as well. Being able to mentor Katy in an art form that brings me such joy is an added benefit.

I believe respite care is vital for foster and adoptive parents. Some foster and adoptive parents we know have family locally. Many family members and even close and trusted friends of foster parents have gone through the process to become approved respite providers through the foster care system. Everyone needs a break and respite care can offer a vehicle to further help a child's healing while being around other safe and healthy adults.

# CHAPTER NINE

# FOSTER TO ADOPT

I began this book by explaining how Randy and I came to become foster parents on a quest to seek out a child who had been orphaned by Hurricane Katrina. Because we both had a great love for children, we felt it was one way we could help after the disaster. We envisioned offering a loving and safe home for a child who would need our experience and care. When the adopted child chooses to participate in their own healing, it can be a wonderful thing. I learned from our own experience and living life alongside other foster-to-adopt parents that not all adopted children will receive into their hearts the love offered them by their adopted parents and family.

I found it surprising that as we began telling friends and family about our desire to adopt, their reactions varied. Some talked as if we were super saints and would say things like, "Oh, I admire you so much" or "I could never do what you are doing." Because it had been such a grueling process for me to surrender to the call of being a foster parent in the first place, I was quick to dismiss the super saint perspective to one of surrender to our next season of life. I had not been out looking for something to do. I didn't always feel confident as a parent of our own birth children. I knew I had made many mistakes and had come to trust that the Lord would somehow make them all work out together for all of our good.

I remember a distant family member saying we must simply be bored since all our birth children were out of the home and we just needed something to do. That stung. Obviously, they didn't know us very well. Randy was still working and I had gotten more involved in creating art, teaching and selling my art. We stayed connected to our four birth children regularly. We were loving being "Pop and Nana" to our first grandchild, visiting her in another state regularly. No, we weren't bored at all.

One couple that we knew from church, Ryan and Rachel, invited us out for pizza one Friday night. Their three children and our four children had all been friends when they were in high school so we saw each other a lot at youth group and sporting events. Now that all of our children were out of the home, we had less occasion to see Ryan and Rachel. It was great to see them and catch up on how and where our children all were and our lives as empty nesters. Ryan began to show his special interest in our journey to become foster parents and adopt. We shared our process so far with them and they wanted to know more. They asked how we were planning to pay for an adoption. We explained that since we were going through the foster care system, it was different than a private adoption, which can cost several thousand dollars. It became evident though our conversation that Ryan and Rachel were interested in potentially giving us money for a private adoption should that be the way we were going, but it was not. Ryan and Rachel had known us long enough to know we were big proponents of not going into debt. It was humbling to know they believed in us as parents and wanted to help us parent more children if we needed the financial assistance. I appreciated the fact that this was one way they could be a part of an adoption although they had not been called to be adoptive parents themselves.

I think maybe the most surprising reactions I heard was from friends who offered to connect us with someone who knew a child who needed a good home. I had begun a Moms in Prayer group for our two oldest birth children's middle school years ago. Moms in Prayer was once called Moms in Touch and focused on gathering moms to pray for children and their schools worldwide for Christ. A few other moms and I met weekly to pray specifically for an hour for our children, their teachers, and school happenings. We became fast friends as we shared confidentially and prayed. Over the years, moms would come and go depending on their schedule and life seasons.

I eventually led a group for the local high school when my children went there. When our oldest, Melanie, went to college, I began a group for college and beyond and continued to lead it for many years.

Of course, I shared with the current group of ladies I met with weekly about the Lord calling us to seek to adopt a child. One Thursday morning before our 8:00 prayer time, one of the moms, Wanda, mentioned knowing a seventeen-year-old boy, Brandon, who was planning to enter the military in a few short weeks when he turned eighteen. Brandon was hoping to be adopted before his eighteenth birthday. Wanda went on to say that he really didn't expect to have much of a family relationship since he was going to be away anyway. Brandon had expressed to Wanda that he just wanted to have a family he was connected with. He wanted to know that someone back home cared about him should he be sent overseas, someone he would be serving for. Time seemed to stop as I began to think about Brandon's desperation to be part of a family before he became a legal adult. I began to cry because that thought broke my heart. Did he really not have anyone who cared about him? I don't remember all the details about Brandon because my mind was swirling with thoughts of sadness, questions, empathy for Brandon.

Wanda's suggestion of a child who wanted to be adopted was the first of many from a lot of different friends and family with whom we shared our call to adopt. The massiveness of children who wanted a home was overwhelming. Couple that with being in the process of learning more about the foster care system that is a broken system. It was a lot to process. I realized that over time I began to not mention it as much to others.

Later, as Randy and I began offering respite almost every weekend, there was always the unspoken questions of, "is this the one?" Or wondering if this child was even available for adoption? I was so confused. How would we know which child to adopt? Our continual prayer was that the Lord would make it perfectly clear to us. And He did.

We got to know our caseworker at the time, Wade, very well as he took us through the foster parenting training and many meetings to fill out paperwork. Although each form and request had a purpose, it seemed the state needed every detail of our life for us to apply to be foster parents.

Randy and I each had to fill out and submit applications with normal information like address and place of employment. We had to provide copies of our driver's licenses, marriage license, our current bank statement, current utility bill, proof of health insurance, car insurance, home owner's insurance, etc. Oh, and I was thankful for the forms for us to get medical physicals. Randy is such a healthy person that he rarely went to the doctor so I appreciated the requirement of a full health examination. Of course, I understood that all these forms and requirements helped the state know that we were not in debt, we were healthy, paid our bills and were able to care for ourselves. I had heard that some couples seek to foster parent as a means of income and was hopeful this extensive process sifted them out.

We had to get fingerprinted for criminal background checks. I had to go two separate times because the machine wasn't working properly the first time. That in itself was a chilling experience as I had to slide my driver's license under the bullet proof window to get a number to be fingerprinted. The same county office next to the city court house that fingerprinted inmates also did the fingerprinting for the state for those applying to become foster parents. I was very aware that there was a reason the workers were on one side of the bullet proof glass and the public, including me, was on the other. We also had to fill out forms so our private agency could request the results of our fingerprints from the state. No issues there.

And then the information requested was getting increasingly personal. I began to grasp the magnitude of our decision to foster to adopt. I went back and forth between being scared and excited.

The forms for us to list our strengths and weaknesses as individuals, as a couple, and as a family were a challenge. Listing strengths felt a bit boastful while listing my weaknesses was embarrassing and sobering. Where were those who thought we were super saints now? Asking Randy and close friends to help me with these forms was helpful since they could offer an objective perspective.

I realized that listing my strengths was not boastful but truthful about who I am. I also was encouraged as I realized that together, Randy and I really were a strong team. Randy's strengths seemed to cover my weaknesses and vice versa. That was a confidence boost.

We also filled out the forms giving permission and contact information so that our private agency could request at least three character references each for Randy and me. We chose a few longtime friends who knew us well, along with our pastor. One of those friends, June, not only filled out the form our agency provided and returned it to them, but wrote a personal handwritten letter of recommendation. I know that because she mailed a copy of it to us. June's words of support meant so much to me personally since she had seen me at my best and also my worst. I still have that letter; it was such an affirmation of who I am and how others see me. Every once in a while, when I'm feeling unsure about myself, I'll pull it out and reread it.

Whenever we thought we had completed the necessary paperwork, there was another form that had been forgotten or a new form from the state or our private agency. After all the application paperwork was completed and our six weeks of training classes finished, Wade submitted all our information to our agency, and it was sent on to the state.

Now began the long wait for our application to be processed. I had no idea that our state had one person running one office to process all applications. The waiting process was grueling as I got back to my normal life before forms and trainings seemed to take over. Doubt crept in. What were we doing? Would someone in an office many hours away who had never met us decide if we were good enough to become foster parents? Was I even sure I still wanted to be a foster parent and adopt? It seemed that not a day went by without someone asking if we had been approved yet. Nope.

Finally, after what seemed like an eternity, we received word that our application was approved and we could begin this new journey into an unknown season. I marveled that the very day we received our official license from the state, was our wedding anniversary. Let the adventure begin.

After many weekend respites, Wade, who had gotten to know us pretty well by then, set up a meeting with us. He talked with us about an eleven-year-old girl, Hope, who he thought might be a good fit for us to adopt. Wade filled us in on some basic information about Hope. She had entered the foster care system around age five and had bounced around a few placements. Her mom had long since given up her legal rights to her and her dad had never really been in the picture. Before our meeting ended, we set up another meeting to drive to the group home together where Hope currently lived so we could meet her.

I am a verbal processer and voiced my excitement, nervousness, happiness, skepticisms, and curiosity from the time of that meeting with Wade until we met him again. My emotions were all over the place. Ever-calm Randy listened well and seemed composed as usual.

We met Wade in a grocery store parking lot near the group home as we had planned. The short drive to the group home seemed long. We first met with Mr. Reid, the same director of the group home where we first began our journey with Wade. Mr. Reid then directed us to the cottage where Hope was waiting. She had been asked to give us a tour of the cottage without knowing the real reason for our visit in case we decided against moving forward with seeking to adopt her. Hope was happy to see Wade, whom she already knew. Hope began giving us a detailed tour of her cottage. I was having a hard time focusing as I kept praying to know if she was the one. I did notice that understandably so, it felt sterile there. It saddened me to learn that twelve children lived in that large cottage, one of six cottages on the huge campus. I quickly did the math in my head. Wow.

I was looking for clues, for discernment and wisdom, when Hope bent down to tie her shoe. Not out loud, but in my spirit, I heard the Lord say, "She's the one." Although it was a clear answer, it surprised me. I turned my head in an attempt to hide my emotions, wipe my tears, and gather my composure. Writing about that moment still brings great emotions for me and I am thankful for the Lord being so direct. Hope eventually showed us her bedroom that she shared with another girl. It was simple yet efficient. Hope proudly showed us her athletic metal she had earned the last week of school and a few other treasures she loved.

Our tour ended and we said goodbye. On the short ride back to our car, Wade suggested we pray and get back with him in a week. Randy and I looked at each other to confirm what we both already knew. Hope was the one for us. Yes, we wanted to go forward to adopt her.

I want to interject that all four of our birth children were in favor of us adding a child into our home. Even though none of them still lived at home with us, they were each excited to welcome a child needing a family into ours. I am so thankful for that.

The first weekend respite with Hope in our home was awkward but good. The next ones were easier. Paperwork had begun to officially make Hope part of our family. Meetings with our private agency caseworker Wade and adoption applications took lots of my time. My gamut of emotions was wide. I kept going back in my mind to when Hope had bent down to tie her shoe and my confidence would again return.

Hope moved into our home near the end of July although her legal adoption was not official until mid-December. I remember the day the official adoption papers arrived in the mail. It had been a hard day as Hope had gotten into trouble again at school. Hope's honeymoon period as our adopted daughter at home was long over. She made it known often that I was not her "real" mom and she didn't like me. I had become her enemy by becoming her mom.

You may have heard—as I had—that if a child is fostered or adopted as a baby or a very young child, they will have outgrown the hurt or maybe not remember the trauma of losing their birth mom. I had heard that younger children will adjust fairly easily to a new family and a new home. This is only partly true. Most babies have spent between eight to nine months in their mother's womb hearing her voice, smelling her fragrance and being affected by her moods, food, and drink intakes. The baby's brain is being formed around the mother's actions and choices.

So even when an infant child is removed from the birth mother, for whatever reason, practically all that the baby knows is gone. And even though that baby is placed into a safe and loving home, they still have experienced a great loss even though they cannot verbally express it. That trauma does remain in their brain and in the body's cells until it is processed and healed. I also had heard a false belief that if you just loved the wounded child enough and taught them what is right, that over time they will overcome the trauma they have experienced. I wish that were true but my experience has shown me otherwise.

From what we learned of Hope's background, she most likely experienced trauma in the womb, which probably continued until she entered the group home around age five. Hope was especially angry at her birth mom even while she verbally put her up on a pedestal. Since her birth mom wasn't around for Hope to express her hurt, Hope took out her anger verbally on me. I learned that that scenario is fairly common if an adopted child's brain has not healed. Knowing that that is common does not make it hurt less. It hurt deeply and caused me to question our decision to adopt and my effectiveness as a mom. I spent so much time and energy offering Hope a stable home, therapy help, healthy food, and unconditional love. I didn't do it because I had to, I did it because I wanted to. I knew without a shadow of a doubt that the Lord had called us to adopt her. Hope treated Randy with the same amount of energy but in an opposite sappy sweet way. She would schmooze up to Randy every chance she got and tell him lies about me. Hope was quite convincing and put on a good show. She did the same type thing with her teachers and my friends. I was being ostracized by someone I loved deeply and was trying to help heal. I couldn't believe this was happening. It felt like I had invited a war zone into my home and I was the target. Once Hope even referred to me as her wicked stepmom.

I kept going back to the moment when Hope bent down to tie her shoe. I knew the Lord had spoken to me even though this was not playing out like the happy story Randy and I had envisioned. Hope was very system savvy, a phrase I use for children who have been in the foster care system long enough to know how to manipulate it and the adults within it. Hope was quite practiced at playing adults against each other to get the focus off her and her needed healing.

Although Hope's brain, heart and soul desperately needed healing, she was unwilling to cooperate with the process. Eventually, Hope's unhealthy choices led to her needing a higher level of care than we could provide in our home. It was an extremely hard decision to make and one we did not take lightly. This was not what we wanted. Driving Hope to the facility and checking her in there hurt me to my core, even as I knew it had to be done.

After about a month of struggling to process it all on my own, I made an appointment with our family therapist, Dr. Jones, who had also been working with Hope while she was in our home. I went feeling horrible inside about myself and the whole situation. I was having trouble sleeping and kept replaying over and over in my mind the unbelievable events of the last months. Right away, Dr. Jones mentioned how he was surprised it took me so long to come to see him. And then he put words to my heart's deepest hurt that I had not been able to express out loud. He said, "You probably are feeling like a failure, aren't you?" I began to weep. There it was, my feelings out in the open. I nodded my head in embarrassment. Dr. Jones went on to say that I was not a failure because I had been an excellent parent to Hope. I had given her every opportunity to succeed and heal. I had loved her with my whole heart. Together, Randy and I had shown her what a healthy home, marriage, and family really looks like. We showed her that she could be victorious over her past and not a victim. We had done our part. We had been obedient to the call to adopt her. I don't have an answer as to why the Lord would call Randy and me to adopt Hope since I believe the Lord already knew how the situation would play out. I only know that the Lord is good and He loves us all perfectly and gives us each freedom of choice.

I love what Shae Bynes, author of *Grace Over Grind*, says, "faith + obedience = success." We were success-ful. I was not a failure as a mom to Hope. Randy and I had faithfully yielded to the Lord's call and persevered even though the result didn't look like what we thought it would look like.

Hope had rejected us and every attempt we offered. Despite our best efforts to give her healing and growth, she chose otherwise. Randy and I are not sorry that we offered Hope a place in our home and our hearts. We also know that the Lord still works miracles and our prayer is that one day Hope will choose healing for herself.

I continued in therapy for a while. I learned to retrain my brain to believe truth instead of the lies I had come to believe about myself as a person and a mom. That was not a quick process but one that took intentionality and perseverance. Although I am no longer in therapy, I find staying connected to other healthy friends helpful for me to keep a truthful perspective about myself. It's part of my self-care.

All the love offered in earnest and needs met by adopted parents and family alone cannot heal an adopted child's brain. And sadly, without healing, an adopted child may even grow into adulthood still grieving their traumatic rejection and loss at the beginning of their life in unhealthy ways.

The good news is that the brain can heal with healthy retraining and love. I found the book, *Switch on Your Brain* by Dr. Caroline Leaf, a cognitive neuroscientist, very insightful and helpful. You may want to look up cognitive neuroscientist but basically, they study the relationship between the brain structures, activity, and mental processes. Her book is fascinating although I had to reread portions of it to understand it. Dr. Leaf teaches that the brain can heal with healthy retraining and love. Over time, a child or anyone can choose to heal or not. Choosing healing is key. A child's choice is not necessarily a reflection of whether you are a good parent or not but whether they are ready and willing to participate in the healing and retraining of their brain.

I have met many children since we began our foster parenting journey who have been adopted from the foster care system and have grown into wonderful loving adults and contributing members of society. I met Brooke and Evan long after they were adopted. Brooke and Evan were not siblings until they were adopted by Kevin and Ruth. Through much Christian therapy and healing, Brooke and Evan have grown into happy, healthy adults and have a wonderful relationship with Kevin and Ruth. Brooke is married now and has an energetic and delightful little boy with her husband. She is fun to be around. Evan is a remarkable young man who has many health and physical challenges and yet one of the most winsome personalities that I have ever met. He exudes love to everyone who meets him. I believe their success stories come from not only being offered healing and the retraining of their brains but choosing it personally for themselves through forgiveness. Brooke and Evan have each chosen to not allow the trauma that began their lives define them.

I also met Eva and Eli many years after they were adopted. They also were not siblings until they were adopted by Gavin and Claire. And also, through much Christian counseling and healing, Eva has grown into a happy, healthy adult and has a wonderful relationship with Gavin and Claire. Eli has chosen not to heal or forgive. Eli remains a victim in his mind and struggles to keep a job. His relationship with Gavin and Claire is strained.

It really is sad to watch Eli and others like him who have not chosen to forgive, heal, and move forward. Their rejection of their adoptive parents' love, care, and healing offered to them was not what any adoptive parent I've met wanted. And still, knowing both of these families for several years now, it shows me that an adopted child can heal, forgive, and move forward to a healthy life if they choose it.

Every adoption is unique as is every set of adoption parents. Our adoption story was not what we originally envisioned it would be. Still, when I've been invited to speak at events about adoption, I always end the same way. I say that I know we were called to be foster parents, to adopt, and to do a lot of respite. It was not easy and often a thankless thing. Still, I would do it again because I knew I heard the Lord's voice. Maybe my experience was to also help other foster and adoptive parents and not just the children. I may never know the whole of why we were called to foster to adopt. People would often say things like, well they are so lucky to have you as a parent and will one day thank you. I'm not a believer in luck but in divine appointments. I have the peace and joy in my heart from knowing that I did what I was called to do at the time. Thankfully, the end result is not up to me.

# CHAPTER TEN

# FINAL THOUGHTS

Everyone's journey is different. The things I learned and ways I grew during our foster parent season prepared me for my current season in life. None of it was in vain. It all had a purpose even when I couldn't see it at the time. Your foster parenting season can make a difference in not only the children who come through your home but in your life as well.

Our foster parenting season of twelve years was longer than many of my foster-parenting friends. I did meet a couple who had been taking in children for over thirty years but that's not the norm. Most of the foster parents I met fostered to adopt because they were unable to have biological children or they simply wanted to add to their family. I also knew foster parent families that just offered respite. It's all valuable. You may one day choose to use your experience to offer a bit of respite to children that have been adopted out of the system as we currently do.

In the end, our season of foster parenting was joyful, hard, exciting, and hurtful at times, life giving, exhausting—and totally worth it. I would do it again because we knew that it was the right thing for us as a couple at the time. I always tell a couple, if they aren't in agreement, wait and maybe seek out other ways to help foster parents. It is vital to be on the same page and mindset as your spouse.

Although, it took a while to see it, I realize now that I personally came out stronger as an individual person, friend, wife, mom and Nana to my grandchildren. Looking back on our foster parenting season, I realize I learned so much about myself while growing in ways I didn't know at the time I needed growth in. I have more compassion and more grace for myself and with others. I found more of my voice to stand up for myself and the children that were in my home. I learned to practice better self-care that also helped me care for others. I used creativity more often as my ally to be organized in my home in new ways. I also found that using art and being creative could be a healing tool for the children in my home as well as for myself. I still offer that to the adults and young students that I mentor through creative quilted art.

I have even started *Art with Nana* via video calls with my grandchildren who live in other towns, states, and another country. We mostly create art together using colored pencils, crayons, and paper. I'm finding that it is a great way to connect and share my values while building relationships with them. We also do art together side-by-side in person when we can. We talk about how art is not supposed to be perfect but fun. I am thankful their parents let them have this time with me to build relationship even though we are physically distant. Of course, Pop Randy joins in near the end of our video call time together. I'm not sure how long this practice will continue and not all my grandchildren want to participate in every call but it is priceless for this current season.

I am confident that many of the books and trainings required for my foster parent license benefited me more than just for my foster parenting season, especially the ones about healing the brain and forgiveness. Some of my relationships have changed but it's all been a growth process. I've also learned and practiced forgiveness for myself as well as for others who aren't seeking forgiveness because it sets *me* free. I am only responsible for my part.

Even though I felt Randy and I had a great marriage before our foster parenting season, I believe it is even stronger now. We were each more intentional in building our marriage to be united as we foster parented children with great trauma. It's true that after all the children are out of the house, biological or otherwise, it's important to have a strong relationship with your spouse still intact. Thankfully, because we did that, I am still happily married to the love of my life. We still date each other, hike, and picnic but have now added playing Pickleball to our time together. Pickleball is a paddle sport that combines elements of table tennis, tennis and badminton. It is great exercise and a fun time together.

We learned that one of the biggest keys to a successful foster parenting season was building a strong professional team. It has the potential to make or break the relationship with you and the child in your home. I encourage you to spend whatever time necessary and get a strong team in place that aligns with your family values. Although it seemed like it took a long time and a lot of effort to seek out the private agency that we felt most comfortable with, it was well worth it. They gave us much needed support. It's hard to imagine how hard it would have been for me personally without that and a strong professional team.

I may never again see most of the children who came through our home from the foster care system. I also may never know the impact of the time they had in our home or if it affected them for the good. They may or may not be at a point in their lives where they have come to peace with their childhood trauma and forgiven those who hurt them. That was not my role. My role was to offer to my best ability a safe and loving home and give them life skills that they can choose to use for themselves, not just survival skills. I am not waiting for a "thank you" from any of these children. That's not why I did it. I did it because I knew it was my purpose and calling for a season. I now believe that I *was* successful as a foster parent. Not because a child chose to heal or not but because I chose to do my best to be a great foster parent and offer them a safe and loving home. I offered them space to heal. I wanted to be like Mrs. Grace, my Sunday school teacher when I was a teen. Even though I don't remember her real name, I remember her kindness, grace, and loving home. Many children may not remember my name but maybe they will remember the kindness, grace, and love while they were in our home. And if not, that's okay. My responsibility was to be faithful to what I could do and grow stronger over time. I gave it my all, as nothing less would have been good.

I encourage you to take some time to identify what healthy self-care looks like for you and make room for it in your day. That has been an unexpected benefit for me personally. I'm still intentional about replacing lies I've believed about myself with truth. Although they have evolved over time, I still read my affirmations every morning at breakfast. It's not easy to let go of what others who don't know me well may say or believe about me or what I have wrongly believed about myself. I am not who others say I am but who the Lord says I am.

Yes, you may need to organize your home a bit differently to accommodate a child from the foster care system. Yes, it may mean changing some of your eating habits and life style but it can totally be worth it. I've learned to use my time more purposefully to accomplish things necessary including rest. I've learned to take respite for myself and recognize better when I need to pull back, rest, and regroup.

My journey will have similarities and differences from yours. We all have different gifts and will approach things in our unique way. You may find that some things that worked for me will work for you and some things will not work for you. You will probably find things that work better for you. I hope you will share that with others.

One of the first teens that we had in our home for only a couple months contacted me out of the blue. Randy and I were driving home from a camping trip and a phone call came in on my phone from an unfamiliar number of a business in another state. Tori asked if I remembered her. Of course, I did! She was quite a troubled girl at the time, angry at the world and doing her best to be mean to me. Tori said she just wanted to call and say how she remembered the time in our home favorably. I was surprised. I remember that time as filled with a lot of conflict and confrontational situations. Tori seemed to push back on every issue. We talked for only about five minutes but it helped me realize that you never know the impact your life can have on a hurting child. What we see is not necessarily what the Lord is doing at the time in a child's life. Press on and stay true to your values.

I began this book telling you about how my mentor, Matt Tommey, answered my simple question on Q&A Day in the mentoring program with a suggestion to write a book and title it *How To Be A Great Foster Parent*— I wrote how crazy I thought the idea was. Crazy or not, I hope sharing my story has been helpful for you and helped you laugh at some of the funny things that happened along the way.

I believe you too can be a great foster parent and go through your foster parent season with purpose and growth for the children in your home and yourself as well. I believe that is why you chose to read this book. I am cheering you on. Remember that on those days when you wonder why you became a foster parent in the first place. I am confident there are others cheering you on as well. Seek them out. Get the support you need in person if at all possible or in combination with people online. Spend time with them and allow them to care for you as well. I found that choosing healthy friends that mentored me allowed me to mentor them as well. We have something to offer each other. Be kind to yourself.

I suspect you are also not waiting for a "thank you" from the children you have or will have in your home, as you know you have been called to this foster parent season. I want to personally say "thank you" for spending this season of your life as a foster parent. It matters.

# AUTHOR BIO

Julie Bagamary lives in North Carolina with her husband, Randy, who is still the love of her life after several decades of marriage. She enjoys spending time with her four biological children, their spouses, and her many grandchildren. Julie is a quilt artist, speaker, mentor, and instructor.

You can get more information at juliebagamary.com.

# ACKNOWLEDGEMENTS

This book would not have been possible without the many people who walked with me along the way.

To Randy: Thank you for being my biggest cheerleader in writing this book and actually all of life. Your steadfastness is a treasure. I love you so much.

To my biological children and grandchildren: You are all so valuable to me and I appreciate your love and encouragement in this project directly and indirectly.

To Trish, my writing coach and editor: Your patience with me as a first-time writer taught me to write what was inside my heart so that others might want to read it. Thank you for sharing your gift of detail and gently prodding me to create a better book.

To Sam and her team at The Cheerful Word: Thank you for believing my story would impact others and accomplishing the technical details to make it happen through your self-publishing help.

To my walking and praying friends: You know who are. I am so appreciative of your continual encouragement and allowing me to process things out loud before putting them to page. I value our friendships.

To the Lord: Thank You for Your perfect love and truth that allows me to renew my mind and have a closer relationship with you. You are the one that calls us to yourself and to tasks bigger than ourselves so that we can cooperate with you for your glory.

CPSIA information can be obtained
at www.ICGtesting.com
Printed in the USA
BVHW051110120521
607049BV00005B/624